Caught Between Truths

The Central Paradoxes of Christian Faith

Barry L. Callen

Emeth Press

Caught Between Truths, The Central Paradoxes of Christian Faith

Copyright © 2007 Barry L. Callen
Printed in the United States of America on acid-free paper

All rights reserved. No part of this book may be reproduced, or stored in a retrieval system or transmitted in any form or by any means, electronic, mechanical, photocopying, recording, scanning or otherwise, except as permitted by the 1976 United States Copyright Act, or with the prior written permission of Emeth Press. Requests for permission should be addressed to: Emeth Press, P. O. Box 23961, Lexington, KY 40523-3961.
http://www.emethpress.com.

Library of Congress Cataloging-in-Publication Data
Callen, Barry L.
  Caught Between Truths / Barry L. Callen.
     p. cm.
  ISBN-13: 978-0-9776555-5-7 (alk. paper)
  1. God (Christianity)--Essence, nature. 2. Paradox--Religious aspects--Christianity. I. Title.
  BR121.2 .C344 2007   2006937957

Dedication

To Arlene,
now separated from me by death, who believed in
the importance of this writing many years ago and always
encouraged me to think deeply and write with courage

Contents

Foreword	7
Preface	9
Chapter 1. Truth—Complexity Is Crucial	15
Can We Keep It Simple?	5
Staying Steady in Changing Times	18
Majoring in Half-Truths	21
The Theological Necessity of Mystery	27
Caught in the Middle	32
Viewing Reality Out of the Fullness	34
The Paradoxical Path Ahead	35
Chapter 2. Faith—So Many Faces	39
The Challenges to Believing	40
Caught in the Tensions of Religious Knowledge	42
Affirming a Quadrilateral	45
Maintaining a Degree of Uncertainty	51
Theology: Delivered or Developed?	53
The Paradoxical Pages of Scripture	56
Chapter 3. God—The Great Three in One	63
So Simple, So Profound	64
The Crucified and the Creator	65
Both High and Nigh	71
The Beauty of the Ugly Cross	76
The Departed Is Still with Us!	78

Chapter 4. Humans—Crown and Crisis of Creation   85
    Two Diverging Roads   85
    Both Flesh and Spirit   88
    Between License and Liberty   94
    The Impossible Possibility   99
    You Keep What You Give Away   103

Chapter 5. Church—Between Heaven and Earth   107
    A Divine-Human Reality   108
    The Church and the Churches   110
    Hate and Love "The World"   114
    Purity and Penetration   119
    The Presentness of the Future   123

Afterword   131

Index of Subjects and Persons   137

About the Author   145

Foreword

It seems strange for a new book to carry a Foreword by a man now dead for several years. The fact is that this book has been developing over many years. Dr. Trueblood, my esteemed teacher, was excited about its early draft and I am confident would have not changed his mind in the meantime. He was a champion of Christian faith that simultaneously embraced intellectual rigor and genuine humility. Such is the paradox with which followers of Jesus are called to live.

Barry L. Callen
November 2006

The major reward that comes to those who practice the vocation of teacher is the joy of observing the development of those students who succeed in making genuine contributions to life around them. To see the potential transformed into the actual is an experience tinged with wonder. This has already occurred in my own relationship with a prized student of mine, Dr. Barry L. Callen.

More than a decade ago, Barry Callen, then a graduate student, shared with thirty others in a class that met in my personal study. The subject was the philosophy of religion. The class became a genuine fellowship of mutual searching. The participants in this fellowship wrestled for several months with the basic question of how to combine reverence with intellectual integrity. I am naturally grateful for the remembered experience. Now at least one of these persons has justified my faith in his ability to think.

As it becomes increasingly evident that the paramount need of contemporary Christianity lies in the field of clear thinking, books like the present one are required. The Christian faith that we prize cannot endure by mere organization or by emphasis upon feeling, and little else. Since, in the long run, the endurance of the cause of Christ depends upon the conviction that it is true, we must produce a team of first-class thinkers who are able to show that their conviction is grounded in reality. But, before we go very far, we must understand, to the extent that finite persons are able, what the nature of truth itself is. Dr. Callen's book is an essay pointed in this important direction.

What I welcome most in the present book is the emphasis upon the complexity of truth. Any questions which can be answered by a simple "yes" or "no" are seldom worth the asking. Because the truth itself is complex, all really important questions demand complex answers.

Experience is both tragic and comic, and the combinations are of infinite complexity. It is no insignificant detail that, at the end of the *Symposium*, Socrates is reported as concluding that the tragic poet might be a comedian as well. Abraham Lincoln told jokes, he said, because otherwise he would have cried. In short, paradox is at the heart of the understanding of human existence.

I commend to readers everywhere, and of all persuasions, this new book that deals honestly with the nature of truth. May there be many more!

David Elton Trueblood
Earlham School of Religion
Richmond, Indiana,
March 20, 1976

Preface

*Don't panic in the face of a persistent paradox.
It may be the only path to true wisdom!*

Christians currently are living in a deceptive and dangerous time. The dangers are complex both in their sources and manifestations. They must be faced and understood for the health of the church and the adequacy of its teachings.

Danger on Every Hand

There are the obvious and tragic things like mass starvation and the threat of military madness across the globe. There are things less observable, less concrete, but just as real and troublesome. A major one, particularly in the industrialized Western nations, is the general loss of values that most people in a society are prepared to judge as self-evident and worthy of regulating their private and public lives. Unfortunately, there is more of "me" and much less of "us."

At the very time when people are talking most about being liberated to be themselves and do "their own thing," many of the same people are experiencing high levels of anxiety and feelings of lostness and aloneness. Some are striking out in violence, while others are retreating into strange worlds within themselves. People are aware that the world is shrinking, travel is common, and communication is instant. The volume of information is overwhelming. At the same time, confidence about whether humans can really know anything for sure is shifting in skeptical directions. In this context, thinking about Christian belief seems to be getting more difficult all the time.

There is yet another danger, a subtle cancer which has a way of eating at the very foundations of the Christian community. The Christian church, in its struggle to be a prophetic voice in such difficult days, finds itself on the verge of paralysis. Christians wishing to mold the times in which they live often recoil with the realization that they themselves are heavily conditioned by those very times. Worst of all, their own faith message and mission have a way of going out of focus. In the midst of the stress and urgency of these problems, Christians too often either lose touch with their own unique spiritual roots or recognize and apply these roots in most awkward and fragmentary ways.

The most fundamental danger facing the church today may be the apparent inability to keep the things of faith *in proper balance*. In the 1950s there was a preoccupation with institutional growth, new church buildings, and expanding membership roles. In the 1960s, just as in American society at the time, the church vaulted herself into a social action syndrome that righted some wrongs and introduced others. The 1970s brought the very opposite, a sharp turn inward, new forms of radical pietism, aggressive pentecostalism, and a tendency toward social passivity—not always distinguishable from outright irresponsibility in thought and action.

The pendulum kept swinging. The 1980s saw bloated economic growth, especially in the United States and England. There was a turn toward conservative politics—mirrored in the churches by a fresh fundamentalism and a "prosperity gospel" popularized by in many self-help books and celebrated by numerous television preachers. One could keep tracking these pendulum swings in the general culture and in the church. The troubling point is that the church shifts so easily and reads the Bible so woodenly, selectively, and in tune with the changing focus of the times. Proper balance usually is in short supply.

This tendency toward abrupt alternations of understanding and emphasis is certainly not confined to how the church chooses to relate to the world at large. It is seen in relation to the church's own most central teachings. There is a frightening selectivity in the portions of truth that manage to get recognized and proclaimed at any one time. A tunnel vision, a halfway theology floods the airwaves and invades prominent pulpits. It presents an open door to religious fanaticism, to basic theological misunderstandings, and eventually to a general weakening of the potential impact of Christians on contemporary civilization.

Paradox and Orthodox

This present book has been written in the belief that both the demoralized "liberal" and the resurgent "conservative" elements of the present Christian community need to grasp again what G. K. Chesterton once called "the romance of orthodoxy."[1] Many major beliefs of the church are actually a joining of at least two coordinate truths that are delicately placed so as to form a larger whole, the higher truth. Very often, the components of a larger theological whole appear on the surface to be contradictory. Nevertheless, each contains a vital piece of the whole. Only together do they form the essential paradox that alone is able to express the real, the whole truth. We Christians find ourselves faced with a set of crucial paradoxes that are *inevitable* if our theology is to be *adequate*. We are challenged to avoid panic in the face of persistent paradox. The delicate ambiguities of paradox may be the only path to true wisdom.

The ancient Greeks typically sought to argue from a premise to a conclusion, proceeding with logical and coherent discipline. Not so with the ancient Hebrews and their sacred scriptures. The Old Testament approach has been called "block logic."[2] Concepts not appearing to fit together comfortably, not forming a rational and harmonious pattern, were blocked together anyway. They were judged to belong together, awkward or not. This biblical way of thinking created "a propensity for paradox," something that fit well into the Hebrew world of the East. However, it is not so easily accepted by Westerners more influenced by the Greeks and Romans.

The Bible is filled with block logic. It reports that Pharaoh hardened his heart, and also that God hardened it (Exod. 8:15; 7:3). God is said to be both wrathful and merciful (Isa. 45:7; Hab. 3:2). Jesus is both the "Lamb of God" and the "Lion of the tribe of Judah" (Jn. 1:20, 36; Rev. 5:5). Other key paradoxes (that appear to be contradictions) involve divine predestination and election as these interact with human free will and responsibility. Which is the truth? The best answer is "Yes!" The whole of the paradox, the completeness available only through certain paradoxes, is where real truth lies. The Hebrews had a timely humility in the face of the divine, knowing that the fullness of truth is not readily available in neat rational packages. They knew, and we must learn, the wisdom of trusting where we cannot fully understand.

"Orthodoxy" in Christian belief means to think both *straight* and *whole*. Church history has seen more straight than whole. To be orthodox is far more than a determined faithfulness to an ancient tradition judged over time as "official." It also should be a determined willingness to approach major Christian doctrines with a broad perspective, with appreciation for the intricate interrelatedness of the strands of meaning, and with a patience that recognizes that there is more to truth than the latest discovery, the loudest voice, the most popular creedal formula, or the nearest crisis. There is emerging a "post-conservative evangelical theology" that embraces the vision of a "critical and generous orthodoxy." Such an orthodoxy respects, but is no slave to church tradition. This stance, as part of its biblical faithfulness, will allow for some reconstruction of time-honored interpretations of the Bible, "using reason as a guide and culture as a conversation partner."[3]

With so many partial truths and unbalanced theologies currently burdening the life of the church, it is time to call for a renewed commitment to a *wholeness* of thought and action. What follows suggests that the wise path is a rooted and relevant theological equilibrium. It is a path requiring some theological patience. Rather than a problem, being "caught between truths" may be the right place to be. Such a place may not be fully satisfying to our Western rationalism, but it may be the biblical and thus the best way to proceed.

Today, as never before, we are keenly aware of the great diversity among humans—and even within the Christian community itself. It is so easy to react by "sectarianizing" Christianity. We resist the surrounding diversity by isolating ourselves behind closed doors of tightly set theological creeds and fixed church practices—it is *we* who are right in the face of *everyone else*. While the diversity may offer needed breadth and richness of insight, we usually choose to fear it as a threat to our own cherished perspective. History is told by the winners, so the truism goes. The most eloquent preachers and clever writers tend to carry the day, choose the memories to be valued, and set the bounds of acceptable believing.

In the face of this human tendency, one theologian has written daringly about the "distant voices" in his own Christian tradition, arguing that "listening to such voices helps one glimpse a modern heritage that is broader, richer, and more diverse than one presently may suppose."[4] There is wisdom in listening to the minority, those relegated to the margin, instead of just going along with the majority automatically. Sometimes the crowd is wrong. Sometimes holding in tension multiple points of view is the path of wisdom.

The Wider Richness of Revealed Truth

The fact is that God and God's ways in this world are understood imperfectly by us. We possess strands of the truth and the inability to see the whole of the tapestry. We are tempted to sanctify our own strands and tear them away from all others. But, it is argued in these pages, our precious truth threads can be all the more beautiful, all the more true, when they are linked with care to the others that stand on the edges of our inadequate thoughts and experiences. Truth lies more in the broader whole and less in the various parts and pieces. What God seeks to join together, let us not try to wrench apart!

Openness to the potential richness of alternatives does not mean that anything is acceptable in Christian theology. The absolute lordship of Jesus Christ, for example, is not open to question if a Christian is to be Christian. Beyond this, however, it is possible, even essential "to be both evangelical and ecumenical, both aggressive in our proclamation and humble in our love."[5] Truth is where you find it—and usually it is not all in our own backyard.

A major characteristic of the worldwide Christian community across the twentieth century became known as the "ecumenical movement." It was a renewed concern for evidencing more clearly to the world the unity God gives his people. The impulse was to champion the essential unity of the faith community in the midst of its obvious diversity. The call was for closed doors to be opened to brothers and sisters who share the faith, but do so with somewhat differing emphases. The challenge was the refusal to absolutize relative perspectives. Ecumenism—and probably good theology—should reach for and rejoice in the *wholeness* of truth found in Jesus Christ and in the various expressions of his church on earth.

Christian believers today must get more comfortable with the wider richness of revealed truth. The intent of this book is to seek theological balance, to hold together what should not be separated, to think and believe both straight and whole (a disciplined and generous orthodoxy). When the fullness of truth is found to lie in paradox, a pairing of parallel teachings, the challenge is obvious. We must find the patience to avoid abortive choices and begin to celebrate being *caught between truths*. To the extent that we do this, the church will become a foretaste of God's *shalom*, a welcome alternative to the destructive dividedness of our world.

The chapters that follow sample the paradoxes that lie at the heart of Christian faith. These paradoxes are identified and affirmed—in their wholeness. Theological wisdom lies in becoming ready to be caught between truths!

Notes

1. G. K. Chesterton, *Orthodoxy* (Garden City, N.Y.: Doubleday Image Books, 1959 edition). Chapter eight is titled "The Romance of Orthodoxy."

2. Marvin R. Wilson, *Our Father Abraham: Jewish Roots of Christian Faith* (Grand Rapids: Eerdmans Publishing, 1989), 150-152.

3. Roger E. Olson, "Postconservative Evangelical Theology and the Theological Pilgrimage of Clark Pinnock," in Stanley Porter and Anthony Cross, eds., *Semper Reformandum* (Paternoster Press, 2003), 21.

4. C. Leonard Allen, *Distant Voices* (Abilene, Texas: Abilene Christian University Press, 1993). 5.

5. Michael Kinnamon, *Truth and Community* (Grand Rapids: Eerdmans Publishing, 1988), 117.

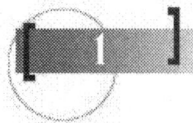

Truth—Complexity Is Crucial

Christianity pivots on paradox. Truth is polyphonic. There are two sides to every story....It is time to land with both feet on the ground, with both sides of the paradox carrying equal weight.[1]

Christian faith provides sound perspective on the ultimate questions of life and death. In one sense, this perspective is simple. God is best known in Jesus Christ. Life at its best is found in following Jesus and being transformed by life in his Spirit and among his people. However, this simplicity is also profound, beyond the reach of human reason.

Faith always is required and humility always is in order. The simple Christian truth is also the complex Christian truth. Religious truth often pivots on paradox. For example, the full truth about Jesus outruns the ability of human reason to grasp and control. Jesus is identified in the New Testament as both human and divine. How can that be? Oversimplification is a constant temptation, the most popular heresy. All of the core truths of Christianity are twin realities, delicate paradoxes. The need is to "land with both feet on the ground."

Can We Keep It Simple?

*It is dangerous to insist on flat yes-or-no answers
to the big and perennial questions of life.*

My wife and I were on a cruise ship in the Gulf of Mexico when she noticed an abstract painting in a hallway of deck six. Its caption read: "My brother just married a two-headed woman. Soon the question came to him. Is she pretty? His response was: Well, yes and no!" The fact is, just as coins have two sides, there are multiple perspectives on most issues. The "and" in "yes and no" may be very important.

Why is it dangerous to insist on simple yes-or-no answers to the big questions of life? The danger is that you just might get them from some people—when, in fact, the simple answers rarely are the whole truth. The danger comes when extremists, who claim to know absolutely, get frustrated with, demanding of, and even at times become violent toward non-believers (those who do not agree with what they arrogantly insist is absolutely true). Their attitude toward the unbelievers usually is one of frustration and impatience.

Allow me to report an agonizing exchange I once overheard. A man in the audience had directed his loaded question to the Christian theologian at the podium. The questioner was impatient and unwilling to settle for anything less than a yes-or-no answer. But the theologian refused to yield to that kind of pressure. Rather, he kept responding with, "What exactly do you mean by..." and "In what context do you have reference to..." and "Have you ever studied theology?" Finally, there came the impatient retort from the frustrated questioner: "Please answer my question! A person certainly doesn't need to have studied theology to understand a plain Yes or a No!" "Quite so," replied the theologian, "but previous study of theology would have taught you that your question simply cannot be answered in the blunt terms of Yes or No!" So goes much of the perplexing dialogue these days between vast numbers of Christian laypersons and the much smaller world of "professional" Christian thinkers. Christians certainly need to understand their faith. And they want to know! But they feel surrounded by real obstacles to such understanding— personal doubt, rival teachings competing for their loyalty, and complex answers from "experts" in the field. Can we not keep things simple?

How complicated does it have to be? With so many "new theologies" currently circulating in the Christian community, one recent critic charged that theological writings seem to be deliberately ambiguous, designed to be taken for either orthodox piety or subtle blasphemy! Whatever happened to plain preaching and forceful answers? What is left in this caldron of cults, this breakdown of tradition, this inflation of words that leaves us with a deflation of clear meaning? Do theologians actually intend to leave open the possibility that their readers can think of them as either daring leaders of a "new thing" or eccentric persons "not too far off the track, if they mean what I think they do?" Or do modern theologians just lack the courage to declare themselves plainly, fearing negative consequences? Or is Christian theology, in fact, too complex or paradoxical for the simpleness of a yes-or-no approach?

We live in a fast-moving and rootless time when numerous theologians are trying to restate the Christian faith in relative and fluid terms that reflect the mood of our times more than biblical foundations. Many Christian laypersons are growing impatient. Cannot Christian ministers and scholars just tell us the plain and simple truth? Do we need to couch things in theological jargon that's beyond us, adding so many qualifications that what is said appears almost meaningless? Please give us a "Yes" or "No!" We really want to know. Will you please instruct us in the *simple* truths of God?

There are too many things in motion today for the average Christian to be able to tolerate much more loss of direction, much more deflation of plain meaning. Since theologians seem to be doing more innovating and dialoguing than remembering and proclaiming, it is getting easier for the honest truth-seeker to listen to the clearer teachings of some strange cult or newspaper astrologist or neighborhood guru. At least such people come armed with all of the answers—just ask them! I am constantly amazed at how the radio, television, and internet are full of "prophetic" preachers who confidently proclaim insights into the present and future which the same pages of the Bible fail to make clear to me. Am I less discerning than they, or are they failing to see the larger picture?

Everyone is talking, but little of significance seems to be said. Regarding the ultimate questions about life and truth, meaning and destiny, it is too easy these days to share Admiral Peary's shock and frustration. While exploring the North Pole, he started out early one morning with his dog team to drive toward the north. At the end of the day he made camp and took a bearing on his latitude. To his surprise and dismay, he found that apparently he was farther south than he had been in the morning. He was thoroughly baffled until he discovered that he was on a gigantic ice flow that was being pulled toward the south faster than his dog team could pull him toward the north! Sometimes the truth is more than what we can see right around us.

This very problem of limited perspective is now shared by many people. Are any of us getting anywhere? Where are the prophets who would be our guides as we search for the contemporary footprints of God? We genuinely need substantive answers about the questions of faith.

> Did God predestine us or not? Yes or no?
> Does God control today's events? Yes or no?
> Was Jesus really God? Yes or no?
> Can I trust my Bible? Yes or no?

The impatience is there. Christian laypersons do not want someone to parade more doubts and strange innovations, and thus burden the faithful with increasingly complex theories and tantalizing questions. They want someone to produce simple, solid, satisfying anchors for Christian believers. Enough of bizarre vocabulary and lengthy theological lectures that strain the mind and risk making sterile the soul. Produce answers. Develop convictions. What often is wanted is a flat Yes or No to the big questions. "No beating around the bush," as my father used to say to me. "My question is crystal clear. Let your answer be the same!"

It is certainly understandable that people wish for plain answers to their most important questions. But what if the only adequate answers to the persistent theological questions necessarily involve the complexity of paradox? What if those easy answers that are longed for, and that readily present themselves to surface thinkers, are much less *adequate* than they are *available*? What if Christian believers, either out of an insecure desperation or a defensive dogmatism, offer pat answers that are more successful at sounding "orthodox" than they are at relating realistically to life and faithfully to the whole revelation that God has granted? What if modern disciples of Jesus, in their quest for crisp and comforting answers, unconsciously sell their souls to a spiritual superficiality featuring the shallowest of answers to the deepest of questions? The changing times in which we now live only deepen the apparent dilemma.

Staying Steady in Changing Times

It is time to be humble about arrogant claims to absolute truth. Faith and humility are always required. We are caught between believing and doubting.

I once heard that, as Adam and Eve were being forced out of the idyllic garden because of their sin, Eve said to her dejected husband, "Honey, it feels like we are living in changing times!" So it was long ago, and so it is today. The current shift is from one way of viewing knowing and believing to quite a new and opposite way. The result is threatening to Christian believers in general. It also is one that Christians cannot ignore, and even one from which we can benefit.

To use technical terms, the shift is from the "modern" to the "postmodern." The first term refers to a general intellectual stance common in the Western world in recent centuries. It elevates science, objectifies knowledge, and relies heavily on human reason. "Evangelical" Christians across the twentieth century drank deeply of this mentality and frequently used its tools in the attempt to demonstrate the credibility of Christian faith to a secularizing culture. Featured by them were "proofs" for God's existence, arguments for the full trustworthiness of the Bible, and logical and systematic presentations of Christian doctrine. But now it is time to think through the ramifications of the big changes that are occurring in Western society. As this modernism mentality is losing its grip on people, how should believers understand Christian faith and go about trying to present it persuasively to the next generation?

Leonard Sweet puts it plainly: "Western Christianity is largely belief based and church focused. It is concerned with landing on the right theology and doctrine and making sure everyone else toes the line.... [However], we may be doctrinally correct. . .[and] become spiritual cadavers." The center of gravity of global Christianity is shifting from North and West to South and East. One result is less concern with rhetoric and reason and more focus on the "mystical," the spiritual, God as majestic mystery, not a divine crossword puzzle to be solved by our wordprocessors. After all, "Jesus was not a Greek, nor was he a classical thinker. He was a Hebrew, Eastern in thought and culture, relational in practice, and mystical in spirituality."[2] Much too often we "modernists" are left with strict doctrinal assent more than truly changed lives.

If modernism (very Western in nature) is no longer compelling in the general intellectual marketplace, what is the birth of the more Eastern "postmodernism" all about? There is no single and simple answer, of course. In general, prominent theorists of this newer intellectual stance are suggesting some major shifts that are making sense to the masses in today's culture. One radical form of postmodernism is a deep skepticism about the human ability to know truth at all. What exists, it is said, is only a host of conflicting interpretations strongly influenced by the contexts in which the interpreters live. We are said to be narrating our own faith journeys and angles of view, but we lack any single line of truth necessarily valid for everyone. This form of postmodernism is a skeptical reaction to the earlier and much more confident modernism.

As long as one believes that the biblical story of God in Jesus Christ is "the grand narrative," the story of stories, the sure path to the real God and the best that life has to offer, both now, forever, and for everyone, the heart of classic Christianity remains. Christian faith should not allow itself to be relegated to no more than one approach to truth among many others, each thought equally valid for those involved. Even in the "pluralism" of today's shrunken world, "we believe not only that the biblical narrative makes sense for *us*, but is also good news for *all*. It provides the fulfillment of the longings and aspirations of all peoples. It embodies *the* truth—the truth of and for all humankind."[3]

Continuing to affirm that the Christian story is the incomparable story of ultimate truth is good, but more is also true. Christian faith needs to shed aspects of the modernist thinking that has marked it so heavily in recent generations. Most conservative Christians have been guilty of an uncritical acceptance of the modern view of knowledge, and need to rethink this acceptance. We have been "modern" Westerners; Jesus was an ancient Hebrew from the East. We have read the Bible as though it were a catalog of religious truths ripe for our picking; the Bible, however, does not present itself as a rational book of scientific or religious thought that readers can grasp, manipulate, and choose to understand at their leisure.

The needed rethinking today will question the assumption that religious knowledge is attainable and certain because of our human capacity for reasoning. Because of the fall of humankind into sin, the fact is that our minds have been blinded, our intellects compromised. Reasoning is not the sole measure of truth. As Blaise Pascal once put it, "The heart has its reasons which reason cannot know."

Questioned also should be the "modernist" assumption that knowledge is objective, dispassionate, and inherently good. The fact is that no seeker after truth, and no reader of the Bible, stands outside of the historical process. We all participate in our particular cultural contexts. Our intellectual endeavors—including Bible reading—are unavoidably conditioned by this participation.

Another important fact is that knowing more does not guarantee progress for individuals or societies. Yes, education is very important and tends to increase one's cultural richness, life satisfaction, and income over a lifetime. Research on occasion does wonders in alleviating or even eliminating some diseases. Knowledge can be very good indeed. It also can be highly destructive, as the twentieth century made painfully clear. The explosion of knowledge will never bring a social utopia. Why? The answer is theological. Advancing technology increases the possibilities of both increased good and increased evil. "Modernism" wrongly assumed the inherent goodness of knowledge. Humans, according to the Bible, are both ignorant *and* have misdirected wills (sin). Because of human perversity, it is a dangerous half-truth to think that solving the ignorance problem will solve the entire human dilemma. Oh that it were that simple!

These certainly are changing times. The change is full of new danger and fresh hope. The call is for humility in regard to our claims to absolute knowledge and our supposed ability to gain such knowledge without the insight available only through faith and life in the Spirit of God. We are caught between competing truths. We *can* and we *cannot* know. Realizing this, however, need not lead to despair. It should lead to caution, to honest listening, to patience in the search for truth, and to openness in faith to the Spirit who ministers in the midst of our best reasoning.

The revelation of God in Jesus Christ exhibits a character that requires believing with more than human reasoning. It requires a realization that faith involves an embracing of some mystery and an accepting of some paradox. On this side of heaven, reaching for the whole truth will be like looking into a heavily frosted mirror (1 Cor. 13:12). We will see, and yet we will not see.

Majoring in Half-Truths

Half of the truth can be worse than no truth at all. To not tell all of the truth is to lie with the part of the truth that is told.

The biblical model is obvious, although not satisfying to those insisting on everything being neatly ordered and rationally clear. The ancient Hebrews, whose thought is found in the Old Testament, features "block logic." Related units of thought often are placed side-by-side, even though they do not make a harmonious pattern. One scholar calls this biblical approach to truth "a propensity for paradox."[4] Such an approach fits the thought world of the ancient East (the biblical world) and is appropriate for the human situation today. From our limited perspective, things do not always fit together smoothly. Rather than force a simplification not warranted by the known facts, biblical authors were satisfied to leave complexities stand unresolved. So should we.

For example, the book of Exodus says both that Pharaoh hardened his heart and that God hardened it (Ex. 8:15; 7:3). Which is true? Apparently the answer is "Yes." The Bible does not choose, allowing this and other paradoxes to stand. Somehow, both sides of such paradoxes are true simultaneously, even though they seem to be contrasting truths. Jesus said that salvation is available to the one who chooses to come, although none choose to come unless the Father first draws them (Jn. 6:37, 44). God is revealed as divine love; but "Jacob have I loved and

Esau have I hated" (Rom. 9:13; Mal. 1:3). Does the loving God also hate? Are divine sovereignty and human responsibility incompatible concepts, or are they both true at the same time? The Bible refuses to oversimplify, to choose prematurely, being willing to accept both sides of various paradoxes. It recognizes that apparent contradiction can be a sign of the divine, the presence of a fuller truth.

There was no compulsion among biblical authors and editors to reconcile the apparently irreconcilable. I recall a famous biblical scholar observing in my presence that he was undisturbed by the little contradictions of fact that the New Testament records about the witnesses to the resurrection appearances of Jesus. To the contrary, he said rather surprisingly, the minor confusions of detail were comforting to him. They suggest that the testimonies are authentic, not manipulated for some editor's comfort. Truth lay in the amazing resurrection happening, not in the technical adequacy of mere humans to report and explain a dramatic event with complete uniformity of detail. The Bible is not recording wrongly, only reporting fairly the complexity of human responses.

A major part of the problem today is that anxious Christian believers are tempted to settle for a piecemeal approach to the content of their faith. One aspect of a subject is seized and represented as being the whole. The result is easy, clear, and readily marketable. Puzzled laypersons and tunnel-visioned theologians, well-intentioned interpreters more zealous than wise, remove a biblical verse from its original context and give it a "relevant" meaning. They isolate a biblical statement from the whole of biblical revelation and thus use the Bible to insist on what may be an unbiblical teaching.

One easily can lie by use of only a small portion of a larger truth. There are numerous church leaders who use Christian vocabulary and sacred traditions in an unbalanced and disjointed manner. The usual result is guilt by lack of proper association. It is the perverted ability to lie with parts of the truth. Heresy is rarely unadulterated falsehood. It is not altogether untrue, just false because the fullness of the truth is missing. It is half of the truth—which can be little better than no truth at all! For instance, Jesus was a real baby, very human. Yes, but is that all? To report only this truth of his humanness is to miss entirely the amazing larger truth of *God with us in flesh*.

A famous poem tells of six blind men of Indostan who encountered an elephant for the first time. Being requested to describe the massive animal, each man examined what was immediately before him and came to his own conclusion. One, approaching from behind, fingered the tail and announced that an elephant is like a long rope. Another, approaching from the side, handled a leg and noted the similarity between an elephant and a large tree. Another man brushed his inquisitive hands along the elephant's side and concluded that this animal could best be described as a massive wall. After having "disputed loud and long," each stuck to his own opinion "exceeding stiff and strong." Sadly, "though each was partly in the right, all were in the wrong!"[5]

Unfortunately, the lesson learned here is often violated among Christians. After protesting Roman Catholic excesses in the sixteenth century, Protestants (protesters) soon began protesting against each other. The result is the existence today of hundreds of denominations, in part the fruit of a Protestant dividing frenzy. While holding most basic things in common, the rhetoric among denominations has usually been "an epidemic of majoring on minor issues," with the Bible being used "to fuel their efforts to prove themselves right and others wrong." Thus, much "Bible study" is little more than "an adventure in missing the point!"[6] As a perceptive critic says about use of the Bible: "Church interpretation has tended to trim and domesticate the text, not only to accommodate regnant modes of knowledge, but also to enhance regnant modes of power."[7] We tend to read the Bible in ways acceptable to our settings and to affirm our own positions in those settings. The texts seem to say to us what we want and need them to say.

When only half of the truth is told, it may be more misleading than to tell none of the truth at all. We learn in Acts 18:25 that Apollos was an eloquent man with high motives and persuasive techniques. But he knew "only the baptism of John." What devastation can be brought by a fervent half-portion of the truth! It is so possible to lie, even though all that is said is the truth. The truth conveys falsehood when it is presented only partially, but with the impression that it is the whole. How tragic when truth is announced in such a way that error is received! Usually, the fault lies at the doorstep of *piecemealism*.

Testimonies of Christians across the centuries witness constantly to the ever-present polarities of Christian experience and to the dangers and tasks made imperative by their presence. That classic prayer of Saint Francis of Assisi suggests the centrality of a series of basic paradoxes fundamental to the life of Christ-like love.

> Grant that I may not so much seek to be consoled as to console; to be understood, as to understand; to be loved, as to love; for it is in giving that we receive, it is in pardoning that we are pardoned, and it is in dying that we are born to eternal life.

George Fox represents thousands of Christian reformers of many generations who sensed an irregularity in the currently taught and practiced constellation of Christian truths and moved to redress the imbalance. Fox rediscovered for himself that an ancient faith has a present tense! Harry Emerson Fosdick, William Temple, and David Elton Trueblood represent others in the more recent Christian community who have seriously endeavored to be *both* intelligent and "pious" Christians—faithful to the biblical witness, truly changed by their faith, and persuasively relevant to their times. After all, Jesus expects us both *to be* disciples and *to make* disciples (Matt. 16:15).

The most cursory investigation of church history reveals that believers have always tended to use only pieces of the truth. With only fragments in hand, they have lost perspective on the whole, thereby managing to make untrue what otherwise would have been gloriously true. Such is the devil's method of operation. In Matthew 4 the devil is said to have quoted Scripture as a means of urging Jesus toward the devil's own ends. Notice that Jesus did not deny the full truth of the biblical quotation presented to him (Ps. 91:11-12). His only retort was to remind the devil that another biblical quotation was also relevant to the situation (Deut. 6:16). The former reference, although true, was very misleading if not seen in the light of the latter reference.

Most of the major councils and creeds of the church over the centuries have struggled against such tendencies, seeking instead to weave segregated sections of a truth into a carefully designed tapestry. As G. K. Chesterton said: "Remember that the Church went in specifically for dangerous ideas; she was a lion tamer. The idea of birth through a Holy Spirit, of the death of a Divine Being, of the forgiveness of sins, or the fulfillment of prophecies, are ideas which. . .need but a touch to turn them into something blasphemous or ferocious."[8] The classic creeds are milestones in the history of the crucial art of theological equilibrium. While many art forms come and go, this theological one must never die! Those with little sympathy for theological precision may be bored with what seems monstrous verbal wars and earthquakes of emotion over fine points of theology. When you are balancing, however, every ounce counts.

A review of Acts 15 reminds us of a critical meeting in the earliest days of the church. The agenda was clarification of a central truth that already was in danger of being swallowed in the midst of competing pieces of that truth. The carefully balanced result saved the church from becoming merely another Jewish sect, one essentially walled off from the larger Gentile world. Similarly, the wisdom of the Council of Nicea in the fourth century after Christ combined several conflicting concerns into a balanced position that has influenced centuries of Christian thinking. This task of maintaining wholeness never ends.

Christian mission is a major concern in the larger Christian community today. Peter Beyerhaus, carrying on the delicate tradition of theological equilibrium, once pictured two divergent approaches to mission. His suggestion is classic wisdom. There is the "necessity of a reciprocal corrective."[9] Many church traditions are now involving themselves in theological exchanges, hoping that there will emerge a theology that will go beyond parochial traditions and do justice to the many-faceted reality of the living church throughout the world. The firstfruits of this process are far from being ripe, but there is growing appreciation of the need to see the whole and not just our personal parts of the whole. To see less is to see too little.

A close friend of mine was shot to death in a senseless hunting accident. I attended the funeral and listened to three different ministers try, as tenderly and logically as they could, to explain to the weeping relatives that God does *control* and *ordain*, but does not *cause* and is not *responsible* for many tragic events that occur within the divine providence. Such coordinate meanings may be true biblical teachings, but they are very difficult to comprehend together, particularly in the time of crisis. Nonetheless, the ability and willingness to grasp this complexity was crucial in that day of tears. Failing to grasp the delicate tension among these diverse meanings would have meant losing altogether one's faith in the existence of a loving *and* all-powerful God. Truth often is lost if *the whole* is not sensed and seized—a difficult lesson for the impatient yes-or-no person!

The ambiguities of life and truth are so very real. We are forced to recognize that our search for simple absolutes, for clear yes-or-no answers to the biggest questions, will lead the careful and honest seeker to an encounter with difficult complexities. Maybe there is no cheap way to avoid the profundity at the very heart of truth itself. Indeed, when dealing with the ultimate questions of life, the *precise* truth often may be discovered in a *delicate imprecision*. Maybe the only path into the whole counsel of God is one of humble and patient faithfulness. Strange as it might sound, there is theological significance in phrases like "a coin has two sides" and "yes, but on the other hand."

Some enlightening lines emerge from the classic *Dialogues of Plato*. Socrates was discussing with Theaetetus the many abstract philosophic issues with which both were deeply concerned. Finally, they agreed on three axioms of philosophy, but only with the necessary concession that there are difficult questions and apparent exceptions even to these basic axioms. Socrates concluded: "I see, my dear Theaetetus, that Theodorus had a true insight into your nature when he said that you were a philosopher, for wonder is the feeling of a philosopher, and philosophy begins in wonder."[10] The closer we come to the heart of truth itself, the more we encounter the magnitude and the grandeur, the mystery, the wonder, and the complexity of it all.

Jesus, in using parables and paradoxes as ways of teaching, outran conventional wisdom. He opened new frontiers of insight to humble disciples who were willing to believe that there is more to life than the inevitability of death and more to religion than rigid rules, stale rituals, and tight logic. Jesus was trying to tell his disciples that the world is a wonderland of possibility not captive to our limited experience. Human knowledge is only a little island in a boundless ocean of mystery. The larger the island grows through study and experience, the longer the shoreline of the mystery becomes. Can we in the contemporary church accept such mystery? Are we committed to the truth in a comprehensive sense, or are we more concerned with finding security in whatever shred of truth we are able to isolate and use to advantage at the moment? Given the stresses of our times, I admit my own fear that we are not sufficiently willing to be patient, thorough, and wholistic in our teaching and preaching of Christian truth.

Jesus certainly simplified truth when he said, "He that hath seen Me hath seen the Father." But even in the midst of such simplification, there is something so profound and overwhelming about the incarnation (God in the flesh of Jesus) that libraries of theology books are still trying to define it. John's Gospel, for instance, is appropriately compared to a pool in which a child can wade and an elephant can swim. Likewise, to encounter Jesus is to encounter the mystery of a reality that is both life-gripping and mind-stretching. In fact, the Christian church, if it learns from the first-century disciples, will be less a group of spiritual know-it-alls and more a fellowship of seekers after truth who have been born anew by the grace of God and have opened themselves in Christ to all that God is and wills—despite the present limitation of their understanding.

Consider that precious hymn "He Is Mine." The words of the first verse say: "How He can love such a sinner as I, I cannot fathom, though often I try." Then come those stunning and stretching words of the refrain: "though it is *wonderful,* yet it is true." The emphasis here is delicate, precious, and penetrating. Truth, when encountered this intimately, shows itself to be full of wonder and mystery, evading the attempt at a final intellectual definition. And yet, despite this mystery, what is encountered is confidently known to be supremely true! It is like that peace that *passeth understanding.* We can't fully explain, but we experience—and we know! The substance of the truth is always a little beyond our ability to reason out and fully grasp; but the substance nonetheless enlivens, excites, absorbs, challenges, and deeply satisfies.

Some degree of perplexing and yet enlightening ambiguity appears to be inevitable when dealing with the ultimate issues of life. We hear in the Christian witness about one God who is somehow three. We encounter a man named Jesus who was both human and divine, and who was conceived in the womb of a young woman in an extraordinary way. According to Matthew 1:25: "...but [Joseph] had no marital relations with her until she had borne a son." We are called to live new lives *in the world,* but without being *of that world.* First, Jesus says, "Come to me, all who labor and are heavy laden, and I will give you rest" (Matt. 11:28); then, later in the same Gospel, Jesus is reported to have added, "If any man would come after me, let him deny himself and take up his cross and follow me" (Matt. 16:24). We find rest as we take up a cross!

One may quote "for all who take the sword will perish by the sword" (Matt. 26:52), only to discover Jesus also saying, "Do not think that I have come to bring peace on earth; I have not come to bring peace, but a sword" (Matt. 10:34). We hear the strange witness from a lovely Christian soul who has suffered much injustice: "Nobody knows the trouble I've seen, glory hallelujah!" We read 2 Corinthians 6 and learn of people who are "sorrowful, yet always rejoicing, chastened and not killed, dying and behold we live!" This is either a strange madness or a stirring symphony that suggests the blending of many chords into one moving melody. It is absolutely ambiguous. It is rationally precarious, and also paradoxically precious.

The Theological Necessity of Mystery

Any "god" we claim to understand fully is
an idol fashioned in our own image.

There is no alternative. Ambiguity, paradox, and mystery are inevitable for those seriously pursuing wisdom in a distinctively Christian context.

Truth is both simple and complex, reachable and unreachable. It is complex partly because divine revelation is essentially personal, and persons have a way of transcending labels, categories, abrupt definitions, and full comprehension. What we have in the Christian faith is less of a cosmic Fact delivering to us a catalogue of facts about itself, and more of a Person, indeed, a heavenly Father who has come to us intimately, encountering us directly along the paths of our historical existence, and calling for our faithful response as human persons to the divine Person. By virtue of God's initiative in revelation, our human knowledge of this Father is real and adequate for our need. But it is so personal, so intimate, so enveloping of all meanings simultaneously that it seems most appropriate to burst into song, rely on poetry, and resort to the use of parables. Religious insight and experience move toward a depth and comprehensiveness that will not yield themselves readily to the captivity of simple sentences and terse definitions. Symbols—yes; verbal prisons—no!

A "god" who is fully comprehensible is not God. This means that a "god" whom we claim to understand exhaustively by our own reasoning and experiencing abilities is only an idol we have fashioned in our own image. The true God, who is graciously near and revealed to us in Jesus Christ (at least in significant part), is also the God of mystery, infinitely beyond our understanding. There are two poles to our experience of the divine. God is *far* from us and *near* to us. In traditional theology, the words for this double reality are "transcendence" and "immanence," seeming opposites that are equally and simultaneously true of the God made known in Jesus Christ. Paradoxically, these apparently contrasting poles of our human experience of God do not cancel each other. To the contrary:

> The more we are attracted to the one "pole," the more vividly we become aware of the other at the same time. Advancing on the way, each finds that God grows ever more intimate and ever more distant, well known and yet unknown.... God dwells in "light unapproachable," yet man stands in his presence with loving confidence and addresses him as friend. God is both end-point and starting-point. He is the host who welcomes us at the conclusion of the journey, yet he is also the companion who walks by our side at every step upon the way.[11]

These are twin truths—and we are necessarily and even graciously caught between them.

The following describes a Christian theological landscape sadly dominated by too many theologian-accountants, theologian technicians, and theologian scientists, instead of by the more appropriate theologian poets:

> The gospel is...a truth widely held, but a truth greatly reduced. It is a truth that has been flattened, trivialized, and rendered inane.... Our technical way of thinking reduces mystery to problem, transforms assurance into certitude, revises quality into quantity, and takes the categories of biblical faith and represents them in manageable shapes.... To address the issue of a truth greatly reduced requires us to be poets who speak against a prose world.[12]

When Christians simplify the theological content of their faith to that which they fully understand and control, they are living more in their own reality than in God's.

A major force in twentieth-century Christianity was "fundamentalism," conservative believers who argued for, systematized, and sought to "prove" Christian faith and biblical authority against the "liberal" forces of the time. Their motives are understandable, in part even admirable. However, the result often was self-defeating. Instead, I suggest that, poetically speaking, we keep the "fun" in fundamentalism, gladly affirming the essentials of Christian faith, but doing so gently, lovingly, with both sides of our brains, with all of our hearts and imaginations—and with appropriate caution and ample humility. The Christian task is not to provide easy answers to every perplexing question; it is to make us ever more aware of a gracious and wonderful mystery, the mystery of God. Rather than an object of our knowledge, God should be the cause of our wonder (Ps. 8:1).

"Orthodoxy," in its best sense, goes beyond holding to the right ancient traditions and thinking logically and straight about Christian faith. It also should be caught up in proper practice (orthopraxy), an active reverence and love for God and neighbor. As Bishop Kallistos Ware of the Orthodox Church of the East says to Christians of the West: "Loyalty to tradition means not primarily the acceptance of formulae or customs from past generations, but rather the ever-new, personal and direct experience of the Holy Spirit *in the present*, here and now." Thus, the Christian life, beyond being a set pattern of believing, is to be a way of life and a way of prayer.

In a later chapter, we consider closely the paradoxical nature of the Bible itself. It is helpful here to note at least the general nature of much of its materials. At a minimum, the Bible is a record of personal encounters with God followed by interpretive shouts and song, narrative, poetry, and parable. Finally, the Bible focuses its whole thrust in the person of Jesus, identified as the *Living Word* who exposes the deepest levels of meaning in all of the other words that came to be written. The whole of the Bible presents an amazing library of sacred literature telling about people who were faced by God and then struggled to find human concepts and language that would contain and convey their experience. Success in verbally packaging such experience was necessarily limited. All human concepts and words are poverty-stricken when they are asked to encompass the being and activity of none other than God!

The mystery of God can be penetrated only partially at best, and then verbalized only haltingly. To know God adequately must be to know God personally through the methods of communication humanly available. God became known to us person-to-person, which was done first with Israel and then ultimately in Jesus. The divine Word became human flesh. But such knowing is only partially susceptible to human understanding and expression. Religion seeks to take us to the heart of the nature of humans and the universe. No simple answer to the big questions is ever sufficient.

Many books present definitions of religion, but all are unsatisfactory because they are short and the mystery of life is long.[13] Apparently, complexity and integrity are related. Those classic words of G. K. Chesterton remain instructive:

> When once one believes in a creed, one is proud of its complexity, as scientists are proud of the complexity of science. It shows how rich it is in discoveries. If it is right at all, it is a compliment to say that it's elaborately right. A stick might fit a hole or a stone a hollow by accident. But a key and a lock are both complex. And if a key fits a lock, you know it is the right key.[14]

The New Testament bristles or, if you prefer, glistens with *profound paradoxes*. We are to take pride in this blessed complexity and not scramble to take intellectual control. There is something about the nature of truth that brings definite conviction without eliminating the element of ambiguity. Paradox nurtures the roots of each major Christian teaching. It is wise to weave a meaningful middle path among the often diverse themes that compose the richness of divine revelation.

Exactly what is a paradox? It is a situation involving two opposing thoughts that, however contradictory they appear, are equally true and must be affirmed jointly if the *whole truth* is to be known. In the tension between the opposite poles of thought, apparent contradiction becomes the vehicle of balanced understanding and communication. It is difficult for yes-or-no people to face seeming contradictions between one's faith and one's life experiences. Some things that appear rationally irresolvable may point to a larger truth that logic is unable to contain.

A recent publication developed for tourists describes the city of London, England, as "stronghold of monarchy and bastion of democracy, way-out crazy and arch-conservative!" Such a kaleidoscope of meanings tells more of the real truth about this city than any one piece of it could. When my son was seven years old, my wife and I decided that, even though we lived in a crowded apartment, it was important to add to our household a little puppy. Then came the paper-training woes, the unexpected fleas, the playful romping by the hour, the cute pictures for grandparents, and the expensive trips to the veterinarian. We finally decided that the whole venture was a *delightful nuisance*. There was no other way to describe the whole truth adequately. It took both words. The fullness of the reality existed somewhere in the mixture of pleasure and pain.

Since the actual truth is often many-sided, it is crucial that we take with utmost seriousness the sometimes troublesome option of admitting the inadequacy of anything except outright paradox. If we Christians would yield willingly to the necessity of paradox when such seems unavoidable, the unsettledness would be absorbed by the sober excitement (itself a paradox) of a basic Christian realization. Paradox is nothing less than a manner of approaching the fullest possible understanding of eternal truths, truths that often are just too extensive in their scope of meaning to be contained in the narrow confines of simple statement. While it may be comfortable to join Job's friends by reducing all situations to "obvious" explanations, it usually is more accurate to join the Psalmist in affirming that "God's ways are so unsearchable."

Refusing the temptation to yield to some artificial simplicity, the paradoxes of truth cling to the principle of the tuning fork. A tone which is musically meaningful emerges only when each tine is in a carefully controlled tension with the other. It is like a person's eyes. As one looks at a distant valley, each eye individually views the scene. But to get the realism of a *depth perception*, it takes the joint operation of both eyes. This principle of paradox is further illustrated by the great height of the Gothic cathedrals. Such height is possible because the central arches and the flying buttresses push against each other. In the resulting tension, there is strength and new possibilities otherwise out of the question. Alfred North Whitehead sums it up very well: "In formal logic, a contradiction is the signal of a defeat; but, in the evolution of real knowledge, it marks the first step in progress towards a victory."[15]

By being *caught between truths*, the person of faith can enter more fully into truth itself. Only here, in the *in-between*, do we have a real understanding of what it means to be "orthodox." Orthodoxy is that theological stance that feels the pull of the competing elements of a given subject, keeps them from flying apart, keeps them in proper relation to each other, and thus keeps them most fully true. Heresy, by contrast, is the inability or unwillingness to be so constructively caught in the middle. Christians should stop associating words like "dull" and "stale tradition" with the stance of orthodoxy. In fact, nothing in the quest for truth is so exciting as the orthodox believer who has the courage to be open and aggressive (not closed and defensive), and who can walk the narrow path with mind alive and heart aflame.

Caught in the Middle

Christians today must be able and willing to orchestrate the paradoxes of human experience and divine revelation into a full gospel that really is the truth.

"Paradox" is an ancient and honorable concept. The Greeks applied it to anything that seemed contrary to public opinion or was strange and marvelous. In this latter sense, the term occurs in the New Testament. It was on the lips of the multitude that saw the healing of the palsied man. "We have seen today," they said in astonishment and awe (Luke 5:26). They knew that there is a depth to truth that often surprises, astounds, and defies the sterile consistencies of mere logic and normal expectation. Much of biblically revealed truth cannot be contained in single statements. Truth often comes as twin concepts that inform each other. How severely the New Testament writings of Paul have suffered because superficial interpreters persist in their failure to coordinate his teaching in one epistle with a complementary emphasis recorded elsewhere!

There are times, particularly when dealing with fundamental Christian teachings, when the use of paradox emerges as mandatory. It is the only means of expressing the broad scope of a complex reality. To be, and yet to be still in process of becoming; to know, and yet to be still in the process of learning; to doubt in the face of faith, and still to believe in the face of doubt, these are clear examples of essential paradox. To recognize such coordinate realities, and to hold them together, is to have grasped a higher reality. It is expressible in human terms only through the vehicle of paradox. Because of this, however, problems frequently enter church life.

Many Christian laypersons and pastors place great value on avoiding conflict situations in the church. But, when it comes to the search for truth within the fellowship of the faithful, there is an important sense in which controversial questions are the only ones really worth asking. Because truth is typically a matrix of meanings carefully positioned in relation to each other, we must fearlessly entertain claim and counterclaim. Only from such serious interchange, and with all relevant aspects of a subject persuasively in view, can an adequate understanding be expected to emerge. This process requires openness, patience, and time.

In 1971 John Van Zanten wrote a little book titled *Caught in the Act*. In the chapter "Existence Between Cultures" he struggles to understand the trends of his time. The question is raised about what it is like to be alive in an explosively changing age. And the answer? It is necessarily a paradoxical one. People express both exhilaration and near panic. There is a rush of new idealism and a shadow of dark cynicism. People today are exposed to more and more information, but they do not necessarily understand more than before. The data is there in high volume, but not the needed wisdom. People stare into a neon-lighted darkness and get lost in one of those lonely crowds.

Today is a great time to be alive; it is a terrible time to be alive. It is apparently no different from some yesterdays, like the one described so eloquently in those opening words of Charles Dickens' *Tale of Two Cities*: "It was the best of times, it was the worst of times, it was the age of wisdom, it was the age of foolishness, it was the epoch of belief, it was the epoch of incredulity, it was the season of Light, it was the season of Darkness, it was the spring of hope, it was the winter of despair." All sides must be considered if there is to be an accurate perception of the real truth of the situation.

One of the more insightful and amusing autobiographies is Sam Levenson's *In One Era and Out the Other*. Among his several bits of wisdom is a fundamental assertion, a discovery as descriptive of our times as it was of his own life experience.

> It's this way. I started out in one era and arrived in another. The trip took half a lifetime. By the time I got to my good old dream castle at the end of the rainbow, it had been condemned and replaced by something more up-to-date in prefabricated temporary contemporary. The times had changed.
>
> I met all the challenges, reaped the rewards, and now find myself with everything a man could ask for, including an outstanding collection of doubts, misgivings, and ambivalences in all sizes.

> I had carried on my back into the promised land of milk and money a heavy bundle of attitudes left over from the old days. Call them beliefs, values, conditioned responses, emotional blocks, or what kids today call hangups.
>
> I'm not sure whether I got here too late for the old world or too soon for the new one. I am hung up between two eras. My hair is getting gray, some of it from aging, some of it from the falling plaster of venerable institutions crumbling over my head.[16]

The painful tension felt by Levenson is not so much that he had to change eras, but that he got stranded between eras and found breathing labored when it was forced to occur in a virtual vacuum. He had been caught in the middle of two truth worlds.

People get caught between cultures and eras. We Christians, if we are insightful and courageous enough, allow ourselves to *get caught between the poles of our own truths*. We are torn by the tensions in our knowledge and experience. Should we close our eyes to a few of the facts and to some of our feelings? Dare we take it all in as we search for the *whole counsel of God*? Or do we fall prey to the persistent temptation to affirm the convenient, familiar, and comfortable, ignoring other elements that also clamor for recognition?

Blaise Pascal's classic words are still prophetic: "There are then a great number of truths, both of faith and morality, which seem contradictory, and which all hold good together in a wonderful system. The source of all heresies is the exclusion of some of these truths...."[17] Even as a musical score may have two different melodies harmonized by one major theme, Christians today must be able and willing to orchestrate the paradoxes of human experience and divine revelation into a *full* gospel that really is the truth.

Viewing Reality Out of the Fullness

Since some theological paradoxes are very persistent, we find ourselves caught between truths.

One song has impressed me as expressing very well some persistent feelings that have been haunting recent generations. The recurrent question asked throughout its verses is simply "Who Will Answer?" People today are pictured as searching for a clue, lost in unharmonized complexities, revolving in apathy, slipping to the edge of disaster, blurting out desperate questions about human existence.

> If the soul is darkened
> > By a fear it cannot name,
> > > If the mind is baffled
> > > > When the rules don't fit the game—
> > > > > Who will answer? Who will answer?[18]

It is here in the lostness of the present hour that Christian people have the opportunity and responsibility to announce that there *is an answer* because there *is an Answerer.*

Christ has answered! His answer is as personal as the problem is personal, as delicate as the problem is subtle. His magnitude equals the mysterious clashing of love and providence, good and evil. He, and He alone, has orchestrated in His own person and promises the complexity of our lives with the comprehensive realities of divine truth. The result is hardly simplistic, but neither is it wholly out of reach. Its complexity is crucial, but not crippling. We cannot "comprehend" in a complete and controlling sense, but we can "apprehend" to an adequate and satisfying degree.

The following wonderful line is found in the song "Understanding Nothing" by Bruce Cockburn: "All these years of thinking ended up like this—in front of all this beauty, understanding nothing." How ironic! The call to Christian believers is to embrace "ignorance," realizing that the human's lot of not knowing anything for sure enables the knowing of everything by faith. Here, in great humility, lies wisdom. The ultimate in life is not a math problem to be solved. It is standing in awe, unsure and yet very sure, thinking of words like "amazing grace," pondering in unknowing, and still rejoicing in the fullness of catching a glimpse of God who is known in Jesus Christ.

The Paradoxical Path Ahead

What follows in the next chapters is an attempt to explore the identity of Jesus Christ and the beautiful nature of His answer. It is an attempt to explore the crossing points of the fullness of biblical revelation and the realities of our present lives. It is never assumed that traditional Christian theology is inadequate. To the contrary, traditional theology is assumed to be more adequate than usually is recognized. It is its *richness* and its profound and comprehensive *simplicity* that must be newly appreciated. If this sounds paradoxical, it is.

The task at hand is to coordinate the many loose ends of basic Christian teachings into a unity, to search for those tension points, the fulcrum of each doctrine where the poles of full meaning hinge and where the only real orthodoxy lies. It is a call to embrace with increasing humility, joy, and fulfillment the whole counsel of God.

We often will find ourselves *caught between truths*. While some theological paradoxes are persistent, discouragement is not the appropriate response. Nor is it an acceptable approach to disguise one of the strands of truth so that all sides seem to be one. Often, in reality, they are not one. They are many. In the very midst of the manyness, however, there can emerge the only true oneness—if with patience we will listen to the answer that is embodied in the person of Jesus Christ. Will it be a yes-*or*-no answer? Usually it is a yes-*and*-no as the variants of truth have a beautiful way of cohering in Christ and coordinating our lives in accordance with divine purposes.

Biblically revealed truth is available and adequate. It is simple enough for anyone to benefit, gaining eternal life now and later. It also is comprehensive and thus complex enough that it is always beyond our full understanding and control. After all, we are dealing with *God*—or better, God is graciously dealing with us. The following words represent challenging wisdom—and a clear warning:

> To accept the Bible in its *wholeness* is not easy. We are much more inclined to narrow it down to a one-track interpretation which actually embraces only a very limited aspect of it. And we dignify that one-track view with the term "faith." Actually, it is the opposite of faith: it is an escape from the mature responsibility of faith which plunges into the many-dimensional, the paradoxical, the conflicting elements of the Bible, as well as those of life itself, and finds unity not by *excluding* all it does not understand, but by *embracing* and *accepting* things in their often disconcerting reality.[19]

Thomas Merton goes on to lament the "reductionist tactics" of many biblical interpreters who use "sleight of hand" to press into their pre-set molds what actually is more complicated, more paradoxical than their narrow party line will allow.

Most people would agree that readers of the Bible should read *the text* and not their own prejudices *into the text*. Even so, the line between textual intention and reader prejudice is often hard to identify. For instance, when I studied New Testament Greek on the Anderson University campus in the 1960s, there were two Greek-language professors, each taking a different view of the relation between the technicalities of the language and the establishing of Christian doctrine. For one, the language was a medium of conveying the narrative history in which

God's voice could be heard. For the other, the subtleties of Greek grammar and syntax were filled by God with nuances of revealed truth. Interpretation of the Bible is often a delicate and disputed business. A little humility is a good thing.

At least one central thing is sure. We have the full truth in Jesus Christ; however, we do not come close to having all of the answers. Faith requires that we rest in this paradoxical circumstance, this knowing and not knowing, believing in the *who* of Jesus and proceeding on our faith journey despite lack of clarity about some of the *whats* of detailed doctrine. The complexity of Christian truth is a reality; approaching this complexity with care is crucial. The Afterword at the end of this book offers some helpful guidelines for the approach. First, however, we trace the core paradoxes of Christian faith.

Notes

1. Leonard Sweet, *Out of the Question. . .Into the Mystery* (Colorado Springs: Waterbrook Press, 2004), 55.

2. Sweet, 6, 9.

3. Stanley J. Grenz, *A Primer on Postmodernism* (Grand Rapids: Eerdmans Publishing, 1996), 165.

4. Marvin Wilson, *Our Father Abraham: Jewish Roots of Christian Faith* (Grand Rapids: Eerdmans, 1989), 150.

5. Poem by John Godfrey Saxe titled "The Blind Men and the Elephant."

6. Brian D. McLaren, *A Generous Orthodoxy* (Grand Rapids: Zondervan, 2004), 125-126.

7. Walter Brueggemann, *Texts Under Negotiation* (Minneapolis: Fortress Press, 1993), vii.

8. G. K. Chesterton, *Orthodoxy* (Image Books Edition, 1959), 100.

9. Peter Beyerhaus, *Missions: Which Way?* (Grand Rapids: Zondervan Publishing House,1971), chapter 4.

10. *Theaetetus*, 155.

11. Bishop Kallistos Ware, *The Orthodox Way* (Crestwood, New York: St. Vladimir's Seminary Press, 1999, rev. ed.), 12.

12. Walter Brueggemann, *Finally Comes the Poet*, as quoted in Brian McLaren, *A Generous Orthodoxy*, 145-146.

13. David Elton Trueblood, *Essence of Spiritual Religion* (Harper & Row, paperback edition, 1975), 6.

14. Chesterton, op. cit., 83.

15. Alfred North Whitehead, *Science and the Modern World* (New York: Macmillan, 1941), 267.

16. Sam Levenson, *In One Era and Out the Other* (Simon and Schuster: New York, 1973), 25-26.

17. Blaise Pascal, *Pensees*, 861.
18. Song, "Who Will Answer?" written by Sheila Davis and others and sung by Ed Ames and others.
19. Thomas Merton, *Opening the Bible* (Collegeville, Minn.: the Liturgical Press, 1970), 58-59.

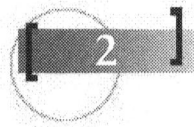

Faith—So Many Faces

The real trouble with this world of ours is not that it is an unreasonable world, nor even that it is a reasonable one. The commonest kind of trouble is that it is nearly reasonable, but not quite. Life is not an illogicality; yet it is a trap for logicians.[1]

When we have finished our theologizing, we shall not understand all mysteries. We are but human pilgrims following the pathways of knowledge, and to the end of the earthly way we shall still "know in part." Yet our faith in Jesus Christ our Lord can give us the assurance of things hoped for, the *conviction of things not seen. And is not that, after all, the object of the quest?*[2]

The journalist Bill Moyers was in London in 1975 with an official of the Saudi Arabian government. Suddenly the news flashed that King Faisal of Saudi Arabia had been assassinated. The official was numbed with disbelief and began grieving for his beloved king. Finally, he responded through his tears with the brave announcement to the anxious American, "It was God's will. It had to be God's will."

"I stopped believing a long time ago in a God who wills murder," countered Moyers. "These things are governed by insanity, or blind passion, not Providence."

"Today is the birthday of Mohammed," countered the stunned official. "God has always used Faisal and it is God who has willed this. Only God could find in this awful thing a purpose to justify it. If I could not believe that, I would myself die." His concluding words of defiant despair were, "Please, the loss of life is terrible enough. The loss of faith is too much. It is God's will. I believe it."[3]

William Barclay, the famous biblical scholar of Glasgow, Scotland, had a daughter who was drowned in a yachting accident. He recounted this tragedy in a BBC program on which he was discussing his "existential" approach to the miracles of Jesus. Despite the circumstances of his daughter's death, Barclay witnessed publicly to the "miracle" of his continuing faith in the love of God, a very special love that was not nullified for him by an apparently senseless death. Following the broadcast, there came one of those unsigned letters from a "friend" of any suffering and still believing Job. Its contents insisted that events are never imponderable happenings, but direct acts of God for particular purposes. It read: "Dear Dr. Barclay, I know now why God killed your daughter; it was to save her from being corrupted by your heresies." Barclay's response was precisely what John Wesley once said to someone: "Your God is my devil."[4]

The Challenges to Believing

When the facts of life seem contradictory enough, all options seem to present themselves for consideration, even the option of embracing irrationality as the most reasonable reality of all.

There they are. Life, pain, faith, doubt, theology, confusion, anger, and faith of contrasting kinds. Eventually we all encounter the many sides of life and the many faces of faith. We are tempted at points to see a lack of meaning in much of it. There are the abrupt, awkward, even cruel attempts of people to capture the "real" and "simple" explanations of imponderable happenings. We also know the unwillingness of other people to force premature and artificial answers to ultimate questions. In one way or another, we all search through apparent insanities for the threads of a divine design. We look back and ask "Why?" We lean ahead and ask "How long?" We look at the present and long to know God's will.

Today, thoughts about traditional religious concepts tend to come in the form of critical questions, even jaundiced suspicions by a generation troubled with rapid social change and quiet personal despair. It seems the height of irony when we observe books on astrology overtaking recipe books as best sellers in public newsstands. The concern for the stars may be surpassing our traditional preoccupation with our stomachs! What should we make of persons holding earned doctorates who also carry in their hip pockets the latest paperback that defines for them in ambiguous, yet alluring terms their horoscopes for the day? When the facts of life seem contradictory enough, all options tend to present themselves for consideration, even the option of embracing irrationality as the most basic reality of all.

When dieting is a national preoccupation in the United States and starvation is a cold fact in many other countries, questions of love and justice should become urgent considerations. What about Christians who live in affluence and seem to thrive on ministry to themselves rather than mission to others?[5] What about the very act of believing when circumstances make believing appear impractical and unrealistic? What about the person who insists that believing is the only real option—even if it does not seem to make sense to anyone else!

What about the many Christians whose honest belief is surrounded by many honest doubts? Does the presence of doubt eliminate the reality of faith? And what about Christian theology? Is it something that we *receive* by direct revelation or something that we *construct* from the elements of our experience, understanding, and believing? If *we* build it, does it have any *divine* standing? Can we know *by faith* something beyond our ability to know by means other than faith? The pressing questions are many.

Religious knowledge is a delicate combination of information, value judgments, and life commitments. It is perceived differently by different people. Paul prayed that the church at Ephesus might "know the love of Christ, which passeth knowledge" (Eph. 3:19). The question is, how can one know with confidence that which admittedly is beyond knowing? In another context Paul announced, "I know the one in whom I have put my trust, and I am sure that he is able" (2 Tim. 1:12). But he also wrote, "Without any doubt, the mystery of our religion is great" (1 Tim. 3:16). Paul knew that God was able; he also knew that his knowledge of God was fragmentary at best. He knew that others could ponder the same subjects and decide that his conclusions were inadequate.

One Christian scholar was re-affirming his own belief in the virgin birth of Jesus. Suddenly, he stopped and admitted that the idea of God breaking into history, of eternity interrupting time, of God cohabiting with Mary, of Almighty God being born from a real human womb staggered his imagination. He continued to believe, but he was newly conscious that his belief went far beyond his understanding. It was necessary that he plead ignorance in the face of the mystery of what God did in the virgin birth. We ask about how we can come to "know" that which is admittedly not quite available to our knowing. At the same time, we affirm with the writer to the Hebrews that "faith is the assurance of things hoped for and the conviction of things not seen" (Heb. 11:1). Faith has so many faces! We are caught among them.

Christian saints of all centuries have shared one conviction. Religious knowledge is possible, even if necessarily allusive and paradoxical. Their very lives have been daily witnesses to that strange process of truly knowing the essentially unknowable. Such witnesses demand our best reflection in a time when a life-orienting faith is so desirable and yet relatively rare. We find ourselves looking for the simplicity of a fulfilling faith in the midst of conflicts that confuse our very search. We must keep ourselves aware of the witness of so many before us who found that for which we search.

Caught in the Tensions of Religious Knowledge

There are chronic problems in the area of religious knowledge. They are the tendencies to lean exclusively on religious faith (Athens has no relationship to Jerusalem), to lean exclusively on human reason (it must be logical and testable or it is not believable), or to choose not to lean at all (it is much too uncertain for me to commit myself). This latter tendency is common in many educational circles where the *process* of searching after religious truth is the only *result* often reached. Whole lives are spent in a perpetual weighing of the pros and cons of any proposed religious decision. It is said to be a matter of gaining sufficient evidence to allow reasonable certainty in the midst of competing claims. But, necessarily, religious questions tested on such grounds remain forever unanswered since the desired evidence can always be judged inadequate. The result is that many are left in a constant holding pattern, speculating about the existence of God and the way of salvation rather than ever reaching the point of personal commitment. These forever searchers are the sophisticated undeciders, the respectable spiritual drop-outs, those who fear commitment or are just playing the game.

Against this process of constant probing and never quite deciding, men such as Søren Kierkegaard and Karl Barth have spoken clearly. No "truth" which is merely taken under advisement can ever become a means of redemption. Unless a person is willing to choose, to take a responsible stand, to leap by faith in the direction that the cumulative evidence points, there is little value in the whole enterprise. Greater than the crime of shallow and untested faith, and these "criminals" are legion, is the crime, the waste, the tragedy of becoming lost in all the testing, with no "leap" of faith at all.

If, then, we must dare to choose, if we are serious and ever expect to really know, how shall we decide what our choice will be? Shall we rely primarily on the wisdom of our human reason? Shall we become persons of faith who are suspicious of the place of reason in "fallen" humans? Or are we willing to take the difficult, although the most appropriate path of the *paradox of faith-reason*?

Some say that the laboratory is one thing and the altar another, that these alternate ways of establishing truth claims exist in different spheres. But this is a false distinction. Any sharp division between them leads to either a barrenness of impersonal scientism, lacking a basis for value judgments, or to an uncritical religious dogmatism that can be subjective, fanatical, highly unrealistic, and even dangerous for others. It is only in the carefully balanced union of faith and reason, functioning in the context of an honest life commitment to God, that we can hope both to know the truth and be free and fulfilled persons of faith.

Granted, faith involves ranging beyond the usual limits of empirical knowledge. It reaches for a grip on the normally unknowable. It commits, risks, and thereby opens a new door of possibility. With such reaching and risking in the realm of ultimate mystery, there also must be an integrity made possible only as faith remains self-critical. This is why there is such danger in the merchants of "nothing but . . ." theologies. *Nothing but* faith is self-deception. *Nothing but* reason is the path of ultimate irrationality. What is required goes beyond *nothing buts*. What must be maintained is a careful tension in which conflict between reason and faith is made creative and not corrosive. Believing with the heart gives power; believing with the head gives balance and sanity. The absence of head or heart brings self-deception and failure.

It is never an easy thing to be caught in a paradox and know that to move from it is to lose touch with the whole truth. Nonetheless, being caught is necessary in relation to religious knowledge. The very nature of the religious quest dictates humility and warns against premature and simplistic assumptions and answers. It also requires taking account of the times in which one lives. The call is not to "go with the flow" and embrace as Christian the latest intellectual or emotional trend. Even so, the context of a believer's life is precisely where one is to witness to the good news in Jesus Christ; thus, sensitivity to context is required if effective witness is to be the result.

The current times, often called "postmodern," appear to require a particular embodiment of the Christian gospel. This embodiment will be characterized in at least the following four ways.[6]

1. More Than Individualism. Especially in the West, we now live in a world where people think of themselves as being autonomous and endowed with inalienable rights. While the Bible does highlight the individual person as highly valuable and truly responsible before God, that is only one side of the biblical coin. God views the individual within community. God is a social reality (Trinity). Faith in God should also be a social reality. Knowledge is gained best with community assistance; individual identity is shaped in large part by the stories and traditions of the communities of which we are members. The Bible makes clear that God's plan has centered in creating a people, a church. Especially today, the public is not impressed with someone claiming to believe all the right things; they are more impressed when seeing a church where people truly love each other and their neighbors in ways the world does not duplicate or understand. The best way to witness on behalf of the church is to obviously be the church.7

2. More Than Rationalism. The time has come when it is hard to believe that human reason and science alone can be saviors of human societies. Of course, disciplined thought and the scientific method of determining truth have freed us of many superstitions and opened many of the fruits of social progress. Becoming anti-intellectual is certainly not the path of Christian wisdom. However, humans are more than "rational animals." While intellectual activity should never be locked out of the church's life, such activity can never achieve for us access to all aspects of God's truth and power. Christian faith is not unreasonable, but it is supra-reasonable. There is mystery that only faith can approach.

Christian faith is much more than reasoned propositions claiming to state correct doctrine. Spiritual experience and interpretive concepts related to it "are reciprocally related. Our concepts facilitate our understanding of the experiences we have in life, and our experience shapes the interpretive concepts we employ to speak about our lives."8 Doctrine is important, although of second-order importance. Primacy is to be given to the transforming personal and community encounter with God in Jesus Christ.9

3. More Than Dualism. The search is now on to find the way to affirm best the fullness of biblical truth. This quest flies in the face of the tendency to dualism, separating reality into mind and matter, soul and body. People today are interested in being treated as whole persons, not wanting their souls saved while their bodies and social settings are in desperate shape and being virtually ignored. Sin is both personal and systemic in nature, inside us and inside the social institutions that we build and then significantly help to build us. Both arenas should be addressed with God's redemptive grace. Thinking in terms of the popular television series Star Trek: The Next Generation, we should acknowledge the interdependency of Counselor Troi and Spock (Data), each a part of us all. We should think in terms of reuniting soul and body, the individual and society, by viewing persons-in-relationship.

4. More Than Knowledge. It is quite clear today that more factual knowledge does not necessarily yield more social good. We are deluged in data. Our computers can deliver a mass of information in an instant. What they cannot give is real perspective, assured values, and wisdom for living. Christian faith surely includes an inquisitive openness to all truth—any truth, after all, is God's truth. What faith should not include is the illusion that the possession of knowledge, even biblical knowledge and church doctrines, is a good thing in and of itself. Paul vigorously rejected such illusions (1 Cor. 8:1). True commitment to Jesus Christ is much more than an intellectual task and an assent to orthodox beliefs. A right head is really good only in tandem with a right heart. The goal is personal and social transformation in the image of Jesus Christ.

Affirming a Quadrilateral

A balanced and self-critical approach to religious truth is helped by use of a "quadrilateral" of interacting authority sources.

We humans tend to dress God in the clothes of our personal preference, consciously or otherwise. We manage to see whatever we are looking for and adapt what we see to suit our own presuppositions, needs, and feelings. Feelings are both deeply human and notoriously undependable as a source of religious truth. Especially undependable is reason, given our human fallenness and thus our tendency to perversity. Christian theologians seek for disciplined ways to compensate for this self-deception and self-serving in our truth-seeking. A balanced approach to determining what is true is helped by reference to a "quadrilateral" of interacting authority sources available for the faith journey. There is a paradox holds the four elements in a careful balance.

Everyone knows that, to score in the game of baseball, a runner must safely touch all four bases, the last being home plate. In the Christian quest for understanding, the home plate is the Bible, the ultimate authority, the place to locate God's revealed wisdom. But to achieve full biblical understanding that is historically correct, currently relevant, and more from God than from us, one must touch three other bases on the way home to understanding truth. No one reads and interprets the Bible in a vacuum. A series of factors are always at work.

The quadrilateral (see the graphic below) assumes the Bible as the preeminent norm for Christian truth. It also assumes that a responsible reading of the biblical text necessarily involves interfacing with church tradition, human reason, and spiritual experience. These are interactive aids to truth identification and interpretation—a written witness to divine revelation (the Bible), a remembering and reading community (the church traditions), a process of existential appropriation (spiritual experience), and a way to test for internal consistency (human reason).[10] Surrounding the process at all points is God's Spirit, who enables all right interpretation, past and present. Knowing is a complex process. We are caught between ways of truth knowing and are challenged to keep them active and in good balance.

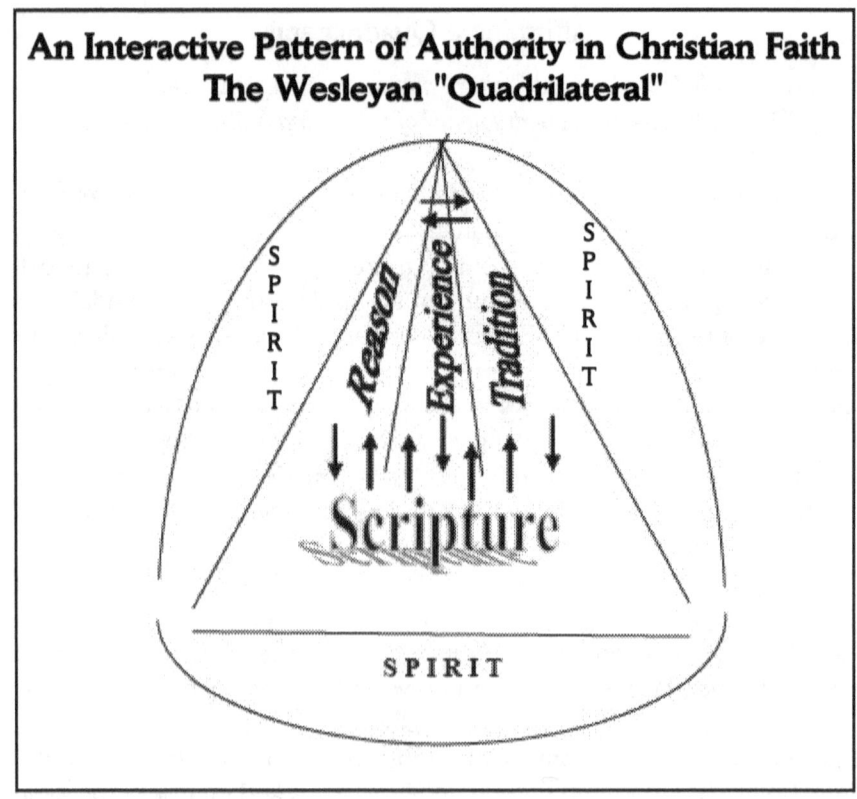

**An Interactive Pattern of Authority in Christian Faith
The Wesleyan "Quadrilateral"**

One tension always existing is the one between reaching out in faith, leaping trustingly into the largely unknown, and working systematically with one's reason and experience to dispel the darkness as much as possible. Which approach should we take? As often is the case, the best theological answer is "yes, both." We should take them all.

The institution of Christian higher education where I taught for many years, Anderson University, has championed the "liberal arts" since the 1920s. A concern of some leaders in the sponsoring church has been that education might subtly supplant the gracious gifting by the Holy Spirit for ministry. So, the institutional slogan for many years was "Where Spirituality Predominates." This was a genuine aspiration of the school—and also a political statement for a nervous church constituency. President John A. Morrison wrote wisely in the school's *Alumni News* in February, 1957:

> Faith without reason is an ally of theological dogmatism and religious superstition, bosom friends of error. But reason without faith is rationalism, which assumes that all reality must be verified, an assumption which is itself unreasonable. This universe is so vast and full of mystery that human reason alone is a puny instrument with which to relate ourselves to it. And the wider our scope of knowledge becomes the more the mystery deepens.

Given this circumstance that calls for careful balancing, a few observations about faith and reason are in order.

Faith Is Required

Religious truth transcends everyday levels of knowing, thus requiring the exercise of faith. There are delicate avenues of knowledge available only to those who spiritually discern, who are humbled, obedient, and listening. Truth, at least the fullness of truth in a Christian setting, is revealed not just to anyone, but only to those few who seek, love, knock sincerely and persistently, and are willing to trust for what is not yet within reason's reach. There is as little justification for trusting the judgment of the irreligious in regard to religion as to rely on the unscientific in matters of science. Armchair religion is really no religion at all. Truth is revealed to the "foolish," to those who have discovered the wisdom of becoming like little children who are able to believe.

There is a sense in which a person can no more "prove God" by exercising logical powers than one can "prove" that freedom or love is real. In fact, the things that count most in life are not readily susceptible to an impersonal, mechanical proving process. They do not require such proof. They can be experienced as real; they are less subjects for debate and more self-evident axioms toward which our best thinking stretches and from which our best thinking emerges.

I doubt that any person really believes in God in a personally transforming way merely because God supposedly has been proven to exist by a process of logical reasoning. Nonetheless, there are solid grounds for such belief in God, grounds that appeal to reason, are aids to faith, and confirm experience. Many everyday assumptions about ourselves and our world are not capable of absolute "proof"—and yet the common person in the street unconsciously accepts them by faith. With respect to belief in God, and quite apart from any exercise of faith, there are converging lines of evidence that any honest person could find impressive.[11] Even so, faith is required in the end.

Reason Is Required

It is easy to dream alluring dreams and spin inviting webs that appear to offer straightforward answers to our deep longings and profound questions. After all, perhaps God is just an idea developed by hopeful humans, a comforting idea that nonetheless is only a pious mirage seeking to sooth the desert of our lives. We must protect ourselves against such a possibility. We are called to believe as little children, but children can be blind and gullible as well as innocent and wise. If possible, we want to know *what is real*, not merely what confirms and comforts us. Although Christian knowledge relies heavily on revelation and human faith, even such revelation must be received, understood, and articulated by rational people employing rational processes. Such revelation, when actively and effectively argued in the public marketplaces (evangelism), depends heavily on the exercise of human reason, common sense, and cultural sensitivities.

Any movement, including the birth of the Christian community, requires some good minds to give intellectual structure to it. Such structure helps the vision of the founders to survive and appeal to good minds who were not privileged to meet them. John, Paul, Peter, and others did this initially. It has happened many times since, including in the early Quaker movement. Elton Trueblood has judged that George Fox likely would have been forgotten without the learned and articulate Robert Barclay who communicated to persons of learning what the unlearned George Fox had discovered. It is one thing to enter the intimacies of the faith in the utter aloneness of repentance and conversion. It is quite another and very necessary thing to translate the fruits of such faith into practical, everyday results that make sense under the scrutiny of the public eye.

William Temple was a prominent Christian leader who combined faith and reason into one abrupt sentence: "Criticism must be sympathetic, or it will completely miss the mark; but it must also be dispassionate and relentless, and nothing whatever must be allowed to escape its universal inquisition."[12] To believe blindly, and be content to rest there in comfort, is heresy. Daring to believe and daring again to think hard and realistically about that belief is a robust stance that bears the marks of maturity. It brings some anxiety to those "at ease in Zion." That is the price to be paid for the ongoing health of the faith community.

The Christian point of view was summed up centuries ago by Anselm: "I do not seek to understand so that I may believe; rather do I believe that I may understand." The Christian begins less with what the human intellect has discovered and more with what God has revealed and we can experience by faith. At the point where human faith and divine initiative meet, conventional wisdom yields to a more profound understanding. It is not "I think and I believe," but "I believe and I think." The difference sounds slight, but in the simple change of word sequence lies the genius of a faith that is open to *all* truth while being controlled by *the* truth.

Once we have recognized these inherent tensions in our human quest for religious knowledge, we come to a very practical problem. How can we know the exact truth about a particular theological question? The experience of life as well as defensible theological method tell us that there is a complexity necessarily involved. Inappropriate simplifying will inevitably breed confusion and error. Patience and care are required.

The ways of achieving religious knowledge commonly identified include authority, mysticism, rationalism, and faith. A good approach is to follow John Macquarrie in listing "factors" involved in the knowing process of a Christian. Admittedly, no factor stands alone. Each is necessary and also inadequate apart from the others. Macquarrie elaborates on experience, revelation, scripture, tradition, culture, and reason.[13] When these are taken together, and in the context of a searching faith, the Christian can come to that deep assurance of really knowing. Similarly, and with an equal concern for orchestrating the several truth sources, Raymond Abba says:

> Authority, for the Christian, is a cord of three strands—the Bible, the Church, and the Inner Light. None of these is inerrant and each requires

the augmentation of the other two. The Church, unless subject to continual repentance and reformation according to the Word of God, is subject to error; the Inner Light unchecked may lead to the outer darkness; the Bible needs to be read in the light of the living faith of the Church and authenticated in the heart of the believer by the inward testimony of the Holy Spirit.[14]

While writing these lines, my young son said he wished to talk to me. He wanted to know what I thought about religious visions. He had heard on the radio a man reporting a vision of angels that had enriched greatly his spiritual life. I responded cautiously. Judging the "religious knowledge" of another is a very delicate business! I asked my son: "What does the Bible say about angels?"; "Have you encountered others in church who have had similar experiences?"; "What was the man's physical condition when he had the vision?"; "Does the whole thing seem reasonable to you?"; and, finally, "Did you catch the man's name or hear anything about his life in general?" It seemed to me that answers to all of these questions were somehow vital before a real judgment could be made.

We are again caught in the tension of paradox. On the one hand, there is "objective knowledge," the hard data, the raw information seen in test tubes and read on dials and computer print-outs. Have you heard of serious scientists examining human corpses and failing to find physical evidence of a "soul," or Soviet cosmonauts declaring that there is no God because none of their missions into space had physically bumped into divinity? Such misplaced investigations are looking for indisputable evidence in the wrong places and in the wrong ways.

There is, in addition to such potential "objective" knowledge, what might be called "subjective knowledge," the soft data, the inner sensing and perceiving that is felt deeply and privately judged by faith to be truth. How do I go about knowing that God lives? Believers often say, because God lives within my heart!

More adequate, however, than a choice between hard ("objective") and soft ("subjective") approaches to religious knowledge is an approach by which a person chooses to be open to the full range of data available in the environment. It seeks only reality and takes seriously known information from any reliable source. It trusts feeling and utilizes faith. It considers all levels and types of information, places them in critical dialogue with each other, gains the courage to take the leap of faith, and maintains the courage to keep such faith strong, self-critical, and freshly informed. Howard Thurman's autobiography is titled *With Head and*

Heart. He says that the recurrent challenge of his life was "how to honor my feelings without vitiating my power of reflective thought, and how to escape the aura of sentimentality typical of the religious quest. . .while giving full reign to that which I feel."[15]

According to the Gospel of John, "The Word became flesh and lived among us, and we have seen his glory" (1:14). To know the truth (8:32) means to be aware of and favorably related to God's saving purpose as embodied in Jesus Christ. The "Spirit of truth" (14:17) bears faithful witness to Jesus, who is the truth (15:26), guiding disciples into all truth (16:13). "Truth," then, refers less to a right intellectual grasp of theological statements and more to a full personal apprehension of the saving presence of God that has come to humanity in Jesus. Such apprehension necessarily involves an intimate personal relationship and responsible action growing from that relationship. Being *doers* rather than mere *hearers* of the divine word is required for gaining true understanding (James 1:22-25).

Maintaining a Degree of Uncertainty

There may be more genuine faith surrounding honest doubt than there is in the process of blindly accepting some conventional creed without question!

In the vocabulary of religion, the word "doubt" has had a bad press. Faith is celebrated as the victory that overcomes the world, while doubt is identified as faith's chief enemy. However, all of us know our times of honest doubt. We Christians have a continuing stake in that ancient prayer, "Lord, I believe; help thou mine unbelief" (Mark 9:24).

Is there any room left for doubting when we are exercising genuine faith? The answer is "yes." The necessary paradox is that faith and doubt always remain in tension, hopefully in a creative tension. Halford Luccock once quoted a pastor who said that most of his church members had joined the church on "confusion of faith." That comment deserves more than a little smile. A real advancement in the life of faith is awaiting many Christians when they finally develop a more realistic and wholesome attitude toward the doubt that they occasionally feel and tend to repress. Faith reaches for that which cannot be known absolutely—at least not in this life.

A well-known European pastor tells of his struggle with the doubt that he knew during the many years that he ministered for Christ. His book on the subject has the shocking title, *If God Does Not Die*. How genuinely this man believed, and yet how persistently he struggled with a part of himself that resisted such belief. He fought to avoid having to admit the reality of this divided situation. But finally he yielded. He could not go forward in faith until he came to grips with doubt. To his surprise, he discovered that moving from a childish to a truly adult faith requires the purifying activity of honest doubt. Such doubt frees faith from the shackles of religious immaturity and the danger of religious fanaticism. "One can, in all good conscience," he concluded, "kill God, for the true God does not let himself be killed."[16]

In a similar vein, C. G. Jung said, "In the second half of life, the necessity is imposed: of recognizing no longer the validity of our former ideals, but of their contraries; of perceiving the error in what was previously our conviction; of sensing the untruth in what was our truth; and of weighing the degree of opposition and even of hostility in what we took to be love."[17] One must doubt in order to really believe. Mature belief is purified by mature doubt. We, however, should also doubt the necessary validity of our own doubts. At that point, one has set faith and doubt in real dialogue, with faith regaining the lead, although honest doubt continues to be judged an acceptable and even helpful companion on the faith journey.

We Christians must move beyond feeling guilty for merely doubting our faith and questioning God. There may be more genuine faith surrounding honest doubt than there is in the process of blindly accepting some conventional creed! There is a degree of uncertainty in faith that cannot be removed—else faith is no longer faith but unquestionable fact. There is a certain "leap" in faith that expresses a person's courage to embrace that which cannot be comprehend, and to trust that which is never beyond the reach of honest doubt. Faith involves risk, calculated risk, a risk that does not deny the continuing mystery. If there is never any honest doubt, it is questionable if there is ever any real faith.

Psychologist Gordon Allport concluded that the religiously mature person will always maintain a certain tentativeness in relation to faith. A mature person has little fear of being self-critical. Only the self-deluded person will insist on holding a faith that is claimed to be entirely above question. Honest doubts can be means of important clarification. They have a way of exposing false securities and even idolatrous views. The sincere person who realizes the helpful possibilities in honest doubt is thereby freed to plunge more deeply into an honest faith. It is all part of our limited human situation and our courage to be humble, even about that on which we are prepared to risk our very lives. As Helmut Thielicke has said so well: "My courage to doubt is therefore precisely the courage of my faith (and not the opposite of faith!), because I know that He in whom I believe will triumph no matter what happens. Though exposed in flank and rear, I can doubt without any safeguard, because He 'besets me behind and before'" (Ps. 139:5).

Theology: Delivered or Developed?

Creeds formulate truth into meaningful verbal packages; always, however, there is a degree of inadequacy in all such packages.

With these understandings of faith-reason and faith-doubt comes the question of Christian theology. How shall we view the creeds of the church? One of the more confusing aspects of my own ministerial education was the emphasis of some of my teachers on "doing theology." I had not come to seminary to "do it," but to fathom it, organize it in my mind, and prepare to teach and preach it. I wanted to proclaim it, not presume to have produced it!

One of my graduate classes was entitled "Systematic Theology." In the very first lecture the professor insisted that theology was not "systematic" anymore. We would approach it as *constructive* theology (were earlier versions destructive?). On we went, first reviewing theology's honorable past as queen of the sciences and mother of universities. Then we began to wallow in the demise of the queen as modern times began to approach her with a tolerant contempt. Even theological students had come to see theology as an obstacle on the way to ministerial ordination. Obviously, the ivory tower systematizer of theological concepts, the rationalistic "fundamentalists," had come under a dark cloud of suspicion. The church had become intent on action and impatient with abstraction. The battle cries had changed. Many Christian leaders now were saying that what we needed was not intellectual exercise, but worldly risk. Only as relevant reflection in the midst of the action could the queen of disciplines regain her integrity.

How did such a radical shift come about? It is a long and complex story. One major cause is easily identified. Scientific advances and historical studies had demonstrated to the satisfaction of many people that traditional Christian theology was, to a significant degree, captured by the cultures into which it had spread and been formed in its first generations. Now that those ancient cultures have disappeared, should not their theological assumptions either be discarded or at least thoroughly revised? Since both categories of thought and styles of expression change with the times, should not one product of the times, theological thinking, change also?

An opposing response from the conservative element of the modern Christian community insists that the problem is only one of language. Words that convey theological truth do change meaning over the years, making necessary the saying of the same things in new words. Bible translations in modern idiom seek such updating. But people do not change; neither does truth. It is only the inadequacy of our understanding, the fragility of words, and the constant shifting of culture that necessitate the regular rewriting of theology. "Classical" formulations of the faith were deeply rooted in biblical revelation, whatever their interactions with non-biblical cultures. Foundational truths have been divinely revealed and can still be presented logically and systematically—so insist the conservatives.

Other Christians, however, disagree. They insist that the challenge is not merely the need to update word meanings. It is the adequacy of basic formulations of truth that is in question. Christian truth is not a body of intellectual knowledge that can be conveyed from one culture and century to another merely by the speaking and hearing of words, no matter how carefully chosen the words may be. Christian truth, like religious knowledge in general, is concerned with the whole of human existence. Truth is life. Christian truth is human life in personal relationship to God and other persons through the grace of Jesus Christ. Words spoken about that life are witnesses to that life, but never adequate conveyors of it. Our hearing of the words of witness is redemptive only as those words successfully point beyond themselves to that narrow pass where God waits for us and deals with us Person-to-person in our unique times and places.

No one is suggesting that formal statements of Christian belief lack meaning. Creeds formulate truth in helpful packages; but always there is a degree of inadequacy to the packages that arises from cultural limitations and the spiritual nature of the truth being defined. A life hidden with God could be likened to falling in love. Theological statements come along to package the meanings for the inspiration and instruction of others. But a treatise on love and being in love are not the same thing!

The difficult question is the degree to which theological formulations are inadequate, the extent to which they must be reconceived and re-expressed in different cultures and generations. Is theology *delivered* or *developed*—or both? One group sees the essence of Christianity in its abiding experiences—astronomies may change, but the stars do not. Another group also gives attention to abiding Christian experiences, but faults the more "liberal" Christians for insisting that "existence is prior to essence"—a thesis that verges on humans and their spiritual experiences becoming the measure of Christian truth. The enduring questions are several. Has the Christian faith come to us in throw-away containers? Is theology *delivered to us* or *developed by us*—or both? As usual, we are caught between truths.

Any serious statement of Christian theology must have some concern for the assumptions and requirements of the present cultural-intellectual situation, as well as some concern for the historic givens of Christian revelation. Theology must move back and forth between two poles, the revealed truths of the historic Christian foundation and the current situation in which those truths must be understood, communicated, and applied. We have seen too much of those Christians who strangle their evangelistic potential by barricading the ancient truths from an honest give-and-take with the realities of the moment. We also have seen too much of those Christians who are so anxious to be relevant that they parade curiously appealing "theologies" that lack a direct tap root in ancient apostolic foundations of Christian faith.

No matter how much we learn or experience, think or believe, in the end there is mystery. The clarity of our human comprehension fades as we move from the relatively certain knowledge of immediate and ordinary experiences of everyday life to the complex questions raised by life's crises and by acts of faith that seek to embrace the totality of it all. In the face of the mystery, we must learn to embrace this essential paradox: *probe without fear and yet believe with all your heart.* Above all, avoid the temptation to short-circuit the circumstance by striving to manipulate the mystery in feeble ways and often toward private ends. The ultimate mystery of life and destiny finds expression in the life of a divine person—and Jesus Christ will not be manipulated! To claim Christian faith is not to exhaust the mystery. It is only to embrace by faith its redemptive invitation in the gracious light of Jesus Christ.

As we Christians try to gain knowledge about religious questions, one thing is clear. By God's grace, there is a unique source of knowledge available, a source that is personal and has taken the initiative to find and enlighten us. This source is *divine revelation*. God, as we shall note in the following chapters, is not some abstract and aloof thing, some anonymous higher power challenging us to peer into an infinite night to see if we can discover something about the distant divine. Rather, God has the heart of a loving and seeking father who has lighted the very windows of heaven so that we might glimpse a gracious God.[18] A theologian, then, is "a pilgrim thinker working on behalf of a pilgrim people."[19] The key resource available is the reality of a self-revealing God. The key location of this revelation is the Bible.

The Paradoxical Pages of Scripture

The Bible is an historic given, a once-for-all revelation that is foundational and unchanging for Christians. It also is a living document that needs to be freshly interpreted and applied to present circumstances and people by the wisdom of the ongoing work of the same Holy Spirit who originally was its inspiration.[20]

The first generations of Christians had the firm conviction that God had spoken in Jesus Christ. The meaning of this speaking was being conveyed faithfully in a body of writing that had evolved among them. Ever since then, great devotion and substantial debate have hovered over these sacred pages. A central problem is that much of the Bible is open to multiple readings; some verses actually appear to contradict others. Sometimes it has seemed that approaching the Bible involves a necessary choice between understanding it as a *human* book, in which the divine element is virtually eliminated, and a *divine* book, in which human elements are denied or at least explained away.

On the one hand, we are faced with a collection of some sixty "books" loosely related and having different authors and editors, cultural and historical backgrounds, and types of literary form, ranging from poetry and proverb to allegory and historical narrative. Much of the material seems to a contemporary reader obscure and lacking in overall focus or current relevance. On the other hand, to the faithful biblical readers over many centuries, this ancient library, now housed in one volume, is known to be nothing other than God's Word in written form, the Holy Scriptures brought into being by God's initiative and speaking powerfully in every age. The Bible is believed to be "inspired," conveying divine truth that has been injected by God into the bloodstream of human experience.

This "inspiring" process is believed to have been God's initiative, God wanting us to know, God superintending the human remembering, analyzing, and writing processes. God enabled each of the writer's thoughts to come into line with God's thoughts. The glorious result is that what was written, edited, and later assembled as the Bible manages to convey the salvation message that God intended. God inspired or in-breathed selected humans so that the written result was in accord with divine intent. Few beliefs could be so central to the Christian life as divine inspiration. Even so, this belief is necessarily complex and always has posed paradoxical truths for which we must adequately account.

The biblical authors and editors obviously introduced into their writings much of their own personalities, abilities to use language, cultural assumptions, and historical perspectives. Each assembled memories and judgments to serve the need of a particular audience at a particular time. Thus, there is a sense in which their writings record something of the writers and their times. The composite result, the totality of biblical materials, appears at first glance to be a jumble of viewpoints on dozens of subjects collected over a period of more than one thousand years of human history and religious thought in the ancient Near East. That much of the situation is very human. But that is not all.

The collected biblical writings also display an *amazing unity* in spite of all the human circumstances associated with them. As empires rose and fell, the continuous story that emerged is of the one God who acted in human history to make known the divine person and will. The biblical reports of this are faith documents, to be sure, attempts by writers and editors to see the divine meaning in crucial turns of the road of human experience. These interpretations were made available to stimulate the faith of others. Such writings gained respect and acceptance. They became known as dependable guides of faith, even as the voice of God coming to each new generation through these writings. The unity of message in the diversity of material is striking.

The inevitable paradox is seen quickly. Real people, limited as we all are by our humanity and situations in life, were superintended by the guiding presence of God. Without becoming merely passive pens in God's hand, they managed, with divine aid, to produce a record of God's thoughts and activities that is reliable and fully adequate for our needs. What then is the Bible? It can only be stated in paradoxical terms. The Bible is God acting as the revealed and the revealer, God bearing witness to God by means of human witnessing to their experiences of God's activities among them. It is the Word of God in the words of humans. As Jeremiah's description of his own work indicates, "the words of Jeremiah. . .to whom the word of the Lord came" (Jer. 1:1-2).

The Gospel of Luke opens with the author informing the reader not only about why Luke had written his account of Jesus, but also about how he had gathered his information. He says that his writing was the result of a process of deliberate historical research. Even though others already had written about the amazing person and ministry of Jesus, Luke's time and setting had called for another telling of the story. In this case, the resulting Gospel is celebrated universally and gives much evidence of being divinely inspired. At the same time, it is inappropriate to ignore the fact that this writing is also humanly produced and transmitted. In Luke's case, true inspiration came when the seeking mind of a man joined with the revealing Spirit of God.

Millions of people encounter the Bible today and have little problem seeing its human elements. In fact, they are nearly overwhelmed and turned away by the flood of translations, editions, conflicting interpretations, and constant biblical references to people, practices, places, and events that are centuries away and worlds removed. Human minds are still seeking to find that place where their emptiness and lostness can encounter the revealing activity of God. They must be helped to see the Bible in its full reality, which includes and yet goes beyond the usual thinking, researching, and theorizing of human authors. Paul expressed it this way: "And so we are constantly thankful to God that, when you heard the Word of God from us, you accepted it, not as a mere human message, but as it really is, God's Word, a power in the lives of you who believe" (1 Thess. 2:13).

How might we summarize the essential nature of the Bible? It is a human record of experiencing God's revelation; it is a written record that is a revelation in its own right, quite apart from the questionable authority of its several human authors and editors. As words of humans, and as work arising from particular historical circumstances, the Bible has a literary history of its own, like any other piece of ancient writing. Such a history can be researched in detail by Bible scholars. But there is more. The Bible, beyond having a literary history, enables new history as it is received and re-lived by people who come to know God through the wisdom in its pages.

The Bible is more than human analyzing and recording. As the revealing Word of God, coming through the words of divinely selected and inspired writers and editors, the Bible is *interpreted* history that enables insight and wisdom from God. It offers assured understanding as well as timely information. The understanding offered relates primarily to questions of a *religious* nature, not to random curiosities about geology, genetics, etc. The Bible faithfully conveys what we need to know for our restoration to God's original intention for us and our world.

It is guidance for our salvation, not a computer program to be decoded.

The main question we humans face is how to gain essential knowledge in matters of ultimate significance. We know only as we experience, as we think about experience, and as we believe our way into new experience, always listening for the fresh voice of God through the pages of the Bible. The person who really wishes to hear will be the one who has learned to listen with the heart as well as to probe with the head. We must come as children who know that being made wise happens only by receiving humbly the wisdom of God (1 Cor. 1:18-31). Such wisdom is found in a marvelous book. It is the paradoxical divine-human book that has survived all critical assessments over the centuries.

Reading properly this amazing divine-human book is crucial. The ongoing ministry of the Spirit of God is central to the process. Here is a key paradox. The Bible is an historic given, a once-for-all revelation that is foundational and unchanging. It also is a living document that is to be freshly interpreted and applied by the wisdom of the ongoing work of the Holy Spirit. Through the Bible, faithful readers encounter the continuing activity of God, who attests to the validity of these documents and applies their insights to new situations being faced. The Bible's truth holds the potential of ever more truth as revealed to Spirit-led readers who live in times and cultures far removed from those of the biblical authors and editors. Nothing that newly emerges through the Spirit of Christ will contradict the historic revelation in Jesus Christ. What once was *infolded* in Christ and the biblical text by the Spirit now continues to be *unfolded* in new settings by the same Spirit. The past and present—we are caught between these, although we are always accompanied by the same loving and interpreting Spirit.[21]

So far as the theological task is concerned, the Spirit of God functions in two interrelated ways—a paradox that must not be broken. One way is to preserve the purity of the gospel as witnessed to dependably by the Bible. The other is to make current that gospel of Jesus Christ in thought, language, and life application appropriate in each new time and place. The church in changing times is tempted either to compromise the gospel to "fit" the times (too heavy on *context*) or to retreat with the gospel in isolation from the times (too heavy on *text*). The Spirit always works toward a right relating of current context and ancient text, the Word alive and communicating now (the always present Spirit of Jesus) and the Word historically rooted yesterday and always (the historical person of Jesus). The same Spirit who originally inspired the Bible's writers must now illumine its readers.

The written Word and the living Spirit fulfill coordinate and interdependent tasks. The written Word cannot function revealingly without the Spirit; but seldom does the Spirit work autonomously apart from the written Word. The Word-Spirit combination must not be broken. Paradoxically, the Christian tradition is both a fixed and an unfinished journey, all guided by the Spirit of God. Christian doctrine, always being revised, develops along the trajectory that comes from its origins. Underneath this conviction is a sturdy trust that the Holy Spirit is present in the church, guiding the work of the tradition, at least in the rightness of direction. Charles Wesley put it well when he wrote:

> Come, Holy Ghost, for moved by Thee
> The prophets wrote and spoke;
> Unlock the truth, Thyself the key,
> Unseal the sacred book.[22]

Notes

1. G. K. Chesterton, *Orthodoxy* (Garden City, N.Y.: Image Books, 1959), 81.

2. Georgia Harkness, *Foundations of Christian Knowledge* (Nashville: Abingdon Press, 1955), 153.

3. Editorial, "Abdullah Wept," by Bill Moyers, *Newsweek* (April 7,1975), 92.

4. William Barclay, *A Spiritual Autobiography* (Eerdmans, 1975), 45-46.

5. This concern is well developed by Ronald J. Sider in his book *The Scandal of the Evangelical Conscience* (Grand Rapids: Baker Books, 2005).

6. I am indebted here to the thought of Stanley Grenz, especially in his book titled *A Primer on Postmodernism* (Grand Rapids: Eerdmans Publishing, 1996).

7. This is a central point made by the book *Resident Aliens* by Stanley Hauerwas and William Willimon (Abingdon Press, 1989).

8. Grenz, *A Primer on Postmodernism*, 170.

9. The Christian spiritual quest and life have been described extensively in relation to the ministries of the Holy Spirit. See Barry L. Callen, *Authentic Spirituality* (Lexington, KY: Emeth Press, 2001, 2006).

10. See Don Thorsen, *The Wesleyan Quadrilateral* (Lexington, KY: Emeth Press, 1990, 2005).

11. These are reviewed by David Elton Trueblood in his book *Philosophy of Religion* (N.Y.: Harper and Row, 1957), chapters 6-11.

12. William Temple, *Nature, Man and God* (London: Macmillan & Co. Ltd., 1934), 27.

13. John Macquarrie, *Principles of Christian Theology* (Scribner's, 1966), 4-14.

14. Raymond Abba, *The Nature and Authority of the Bible* (Muhlenberg Press, 1958), 307-308.

15. Howard Thurman, *With Head and Heart* (Harcourt Brace Jovanovich, 1979), 226.

16. Bernard Martin, *If God Does Not Die* (John Knox Press, 1964), 19.

17. Martin, Preface.

18. For an extensive study of the various ways that Christians have sought to understand God over the centuries, see Barry L. Callen, *Discerning the Divine* (Louisville: Westminster John Knox Press, 2004).

19. Stanley Grenz, *Revisioning Evanglical Theology* (Downers Grove, Ill.: InterVarsity Press, 1993), 83.

20. See Clark Pinnock and Barry Callen, *The Scripture Principle* (Grand Rapids: Baker Academic, 2006), for an extensive discussion of this subject.

21. For a full development of these thoughts, see Pinnock and Callen, *The Scripture Principle*, chaps. 7–8.

22. Charles Wesley, as quoted by T. Crichton Mitchell, *Charles Wesley: Man with the Dancing Heart* (Kansas City: Beacon Hill Press, 1994), 137-138.

God—the Great Three in One

When we speak of the Trinity, we express our belief in the one God who is not a solitary being, but a communion in love characterized by overflowing life. The Trinity is. . .a symbol that points to a three-folded relationality in God. It speaks of shared life at the heart of the universe and establishes mutual relationship as the paradigm for personal and social life.[1]

We have established that Christian believing is an urgent and delicate process, one that can be both frustrating and fulfilling. It is a process that transcends our human reason, although faith is not itself unreasonable. The believing process dares to risk all, even though an element of uncertainty always persists. In light of this, it is time to consider the basic teachings that make up the very core of traditional Christian belief.

Our general thesis remains. At the heart of each major Christian teaching we will discover a cluster of meanings that creates an evident paradox. Our willingness to understand and affirm the entirety of these paradoxes is crucial. In them alone lies strength, adequacy, and the only real truth. Each Christian truth is really a group of related truths held in balance. Only as we are caught up among them and move with their ebb and flow will we ever be enabled to approach an understanding of the larger truth. Like the ancient Hebrews, being caught between truths might sometimes be an uncomfortable experience, but it can be enriching and enabling—and it is the only place to be. In fact, the path of paradox is the biblically revealed path of wisdom.

Let us begin with the most fundamental of all beliefs, the Christian's distinctive approach to understanding God. This understanding is commonly known as the doctrine of the Trinity. If ever something looked designed to confuse the wisest of seekers after truth, here it is. God is one, although in some sense God is three. Christianity is strictly monotheistic (belief in only one God), but it nonetheless affirms a multiplicity related to the very nature of God. God, who exists alone, is not a solitary being. There is the marvelous mystery of a three-fold relationality within the very being of God. Christian faith rests on this fundamental paradox, the one God who somehow is three.

So Simple, So Profound

Speaking of a "Triune" God is not an unnecessary complication of the truth; it is the best way to hold together a series of interlocking truths.

Surprisingly, it was a Christian theologian, Martin Luther, who was named "Man of the Millennium" in the year 2000. He was judged the most influential human to live in the last 1,000 years! A biographer of Luther notes that the grand themes of his life involved "the proper dealing with a God of wrath and love, and the search for certitude in God's relation to humans." Luther had an "obsession with God: God present and God absent, God too near and God too far, the God of wrath and the God of love, God weak and God almighty, God real and God as illusion, God hidden and God revealed."[2] Christian faith begins with the God whose nature is understood to be a mystery, an amazement, even an enigma.

No wonder so many Christians give up in their attempts to understand traditional Christian theology. After kneeling in contrition and literally weeping their way into new life in Jesus Christ, babes in the faith are faced with the awesome task of thinking seriously about the truths that establish their new citizenship in the kingdom of God. The first reads like a riddle. Theology can leave one spiritually chilled if what is communicated is a cold, intellectual formulation, an apparent manipulation of some abstract ideas that appear inaccessible and even contradictory. The all-powerful God of the universe is said to be known best as a helpless baby in an isolated Palestinian barn. The one and only God is somehow also three. Our hearts cry out for God, but not for perplexing theological formulas that seem to obscure the divine!

The fact is that human minds are so small and God's being is so vast. We reach out for the most comprehensive of all things, hoping that God will be available, understandable, clarifying and not confusing. Many of us are deafened by the noise of church business operations. Occasionally we are disgusted by the momentary attraction we have to our own pet ideas and private idolatries. What we are ready for is the good news of God. But we are faced with a demanding reality. It is obvious that it will take some precision and patience to keep this good news free from distortion. There are interlocking truths and we are caught in the middle of them.

To begin, the Christian doctrine of the Triune God seeks to express the fullness of the divine being as God stands self-revealed to us. This trinitarianism is a foundational piece of traditional theology. It is not trying to complicate the truth; rather, it is a tested and proven way of holding together a series of truths which, only in their togetherness, bring into focus the wholly adequate approach to God. It is so simple, and yet so profound.

The occurrence of this complex doctrine of the Trinity is at least implied in Paul's famous benediction to the church in Corinth (2 Cor. 13:14). This suggests that the doctrine emerged from the riches of the spiritual pilgrimages of inspired Christian saints. Such people had been privileged to encounter God personally and had found that no descriptive words about God were adequate unless, at a minimum, they included "Father, Son, and Holy Spirit." What they knew about God through historical event and personal experience demanded such a breadth of affirmation. For them, truly knowing God began with knowing the story of Jesus. The universal was illuminated best in this particular man.

The Crucified and the Creator

It is quite a claim to make for a baby. He was born in a barn to very poor parents, and yet was both fully human and fully divine!

It is significant that Paul's reference to the triune God (2 Cor. 13:13) begins with "the grace of the Lord Jesus Christ." The dynamic of the Christian movement and of its understanding of God originated in the life of a real man and the impact of his teachings, death, and resurrection on the re-born lives of his followers. The basic concept of God came to those first "Christians" from lived, grace-filled observation and experience, not from philosophic speculation.

At Caesarea Philippi, Jesus asked his disciples the greatest of his questions and offered a ringing challenge. Here was a dramatic setting and strange set of circumstances. First, a wandering Galilean preacher was addressing a little company of uneducated, poor, and common men, while the religious authorities were scheming to bring about his death as a dangerous heretic and disturber of the peace. Next was the place itself, filled with the memories of the ancient gods of Canaan, a place where people had worshipped the gods of Greece, and now where the white splendor of a magnificent temple marked the majesty of imperial Rome. Finally, there was the apparent awkwardness of Jesus asking a question that invited an answer that would be nothing short of identifying himself as the Son of God!

All of this seems fictional, highly unlikely, a misguided man with an over-extended ego. He was addressing a set of handpicked friends who were genuinely convinced by it all. But those pagan gods of Canaan, Greece, and Rome are now gone, those ancient kingdoms are barely remembered, and that Jesus is nothing less than a 2,000-year-old, twenty-first century phenomenon! Whatever one may think about the reported miracles of Jesus, he himself should be seen as the greatest miracle of all. Some explanation must be found for the fact that Jesus began as a peasant woman's "illegitimate" child, born in an out-of-the-way corner of the ancient world, and then emerged as the holder of a foremost place in the massive stream of human history. Regardless of how humble the beginnings, it is this striking consequence that demands our attention and invites our admiration, and even worship. Who was—is—this amazing man from Nazareth? Can it be true that knowing him is the best way to approach knowing God?

Jesus must have had considerable personal charm. People with real prejudice against him, like the woman of Samaria or the officers sent by the priests to arrest him, listened to him in spite of themselves. The woman told him all about herself and rushed to tell others of the integrity, perception, and gentleness of this most unusual man. The officers fell under his spell and went back to Jerusalem flatly refusing to carry out orders against him. Jesus became a very popular dinner guest in Jerusalem. Children apparently delighted in him, and even some sinners seemed to be so comfortable around him that the resulting rumors verged on being scandalous in the eyes of the Jewish religious authorities. Many of Jesus' first disciples probably did not begin to follow him because he was believed to be the Messiah (some were not sure of that after three years of being with him). They tended to follow initially because he was an attractive and compelling person who talked sense, had courage, and taught with an authority not present in other teachers.

Jesus once could and still can be misunderstood easily—just an eccentric preacher, a clever revolutionary who was not clever enough to avoid execution, the founder of another of the world's many religions, or a noble soul whose idealistic ideas will not work in our kind of world. Strangely enough, Jesus often seemed to wrap himself in an evasive cloak of secrecy concerning his real identity, almost as though he wanted to remain ambiguous and always on the verge of being misunderstood. For some reason, he called on people to search for him. His real identity could not be gained cheaply. It cost each potential disciple a certain agony and obedience, mixed with a persistency in knocking and believing. It has always taken faith to grasp the real person of Jesus. Required of every aspiring believer is the enlightening initiative of God and the wisdom that only comes from spending time with Jesus on the road of life.

Who is Jesus? Christians know who he is mainly by faith in the accuracy of historic creedal statements of the church and in the pivotal historic events on which such creeds are based. But Christians also come to really know Jesus only as they choose to walk humbly in his way. Albert Schweitzer once concluded that, with the sources available to us, we cannot know for sure the real identity of the historical Jesus. Even so, he pointed in a helpful direction with these classic words:

> He [Jesus] comes to us as One unknown, without a name, as of old by the lakeside He came to those who knew Him not. He speaks to us the same word, "Follow thou Me," and sets us to the task which He has to fulfill for our time. He commands. And to those who obey Him, whether they be wise or simple, He will reveal Himself in the toils, the conflicts, the sufferings which they shall pass through in His fellowship, and, as an ineffable mystery, they shall learn in their own experience who He is.[3]

When Peter confessed that he knew who he really was, Jesus replied, "Flesh and blood has not revealed this to you, but my Father who is in heaven" (Matt. 16:17). The basic requirements for knowing apparently are searching with an honest longing to know the truth, being willing to add time, toil, and faith to the quest, and realizing that, in the end, this God-man, Jesus, becomes known only as God chooses to Self-reveal. "When you seek me with all your heart," says God's own commentary on the matter, "I will be found by you" (Jer. 29:13-14).

There it is! The central teaching of the Christian faith is simply this. *Recognizing Jesus is tantamount to knowing God.* Discovering the identity of Jesus is actually *being found by God.* The four Gospels in the New Testament are laden with references to disciples who were filled with awe as they looked at Jesus through the eyes of faith and became convinced that they were seeing nothing less than God becoming known to them in a saving way. One of the more remarkable facts in the whole history of religious thought is this: when the early Christians reflected on the dreadful realities of the crucifixion of Jesus, it made them think of the redeeming love of God. The cross was not merely the sacrifice and compassion of Jesus; it was *the eternal love of God in action on their behalf.* To see the crucified one was to glimpse the very heart of God. This is the heart of the Christian faith.

Paul acquired the ability to endure threats and tragedies of all kinds, while still believing that nothing "shall be able to separate us from the love of God, which is in Christ Jesus our Lord" (Rom. 8:39). He taught the Corinthians that "Jesus Christ...was not yes and no; but in Him it is always Yes. For all the promises of God find their Yes in Him" (2 Cor. 1:19-20). By faith in the person and work of Jesus, we lost humans finally come to know with confidence that God is love actively finding us.

The evidence collected by fragile humans is always yes and no, God does exist and God does not, God is love and God is not. The harsh facts of life leave us caught between many apparent truths. But, in Jesus the Christ, we see by faith the ultimate Yes beyond the constant paralysis of our yes-no human conclusions. We finally see clearly because, in Jesus Christ, God has chosen to be revealed in a manner comprehensible to our human ways of experiencing and understanding. The need for faith is not removed. What is introduced is a concrete focus of the divine, provided by divine initiative. It enables a definitive reference point that rewards our search for God with assured perspective.

It is vitally important to be aware that the question of the true identity of Jesus is not exhausted by our inquiries into his psychological development, how his mind worked, when and to what extent he was conscious of an "otherness" about himself, even what specific theological claims he made about himself and his mission. From an historical viewpoint, it seems justified to assume that Jesus was (is) the climax of humankind's age-long quest for God. In one sense, he is the pioneer of our faith, the supreme spiritual pathfinder, the greatest of all believers, the unparalleled discoverer of the true and living God. If he were not at least all of these things, he could not be more than these, and he would hardly deserve our admiration, let alone our worship. But if Jesus were (is) at least all of these things, then the God whose true nature Jesus has made known is no less than the One who has been seeking us and who, at his own initiative and by his own grace, has finally and fully reached us and been with us *in this man Jesus.*

We all lead busy lives. Most of us prefer to keep things as simple as possible. But the facts of this situation defy any artificial simplicity. When we truly believe in the man Jesus and in the adequacy of his teachings about God, we are forced by sheer logic to a consideration of

"Christology," that is, thinking seriously about the identity of Jesus in relation to the being of God. Jesus was a man who somehow also *was God being present and active in our world*. D. M. Baillie concludes: "The whole story in the Bible suggests not so much phrases like 'human quest' as phrases like 'divine revelation.'... And if that long story represents reality, and if Jesus truly was the climax of it...then there must be something further to be said about Jesus than that He was the supreme discoverer of God....We must pass beyond words like 'discovery' and even 'revelation' to words like 'incarnation.'"[4] Incarnation means nothing less than that in the flesh of Jesus there was the active presence of God.

In Jesus, we are enabled to see far more than the highest-reaching human hand, the hand that stretches farthest across the gulf to touch the Father's hand. What we see in Jesus is also the outstretched hand of the Father reaching in love toward us! At best, we are people who must toil upward in the quest for truth and happiness. However, Jesus came from the side where fulfillment is already known. He was more than *in touch* with truth. In some mysterious, beautiful, and complex way, He *was* the truth. Jesus was more than the One who spoke peace and even the waves were still. He *was* the peace that passes our understanding and brings sanity to our world. He was more than in direct touch with the Father. He and the Father were somehow *really one*. Here is the paradox of all paradoxes, the heart of Christian faith. We are caught between the coordinate truths of the humanity and divinity of Jesus.

When speaking of Jesus, we are privileged to conclude that we are also and necessarily talking about the One whose arms encompass time and eternity like giant parentheses. In Jesus, we speak about the One who, being both alpha and omega, is the full alphabet of meaning itself. We are talking about God! God had become flesh and dwelt among us—as one of us (Jn. 1:14). Martin Luther once tried to state this amazing paradox: Jesus "lies as a child in Mary's lap, although the universe cannot contain him." Indeed, that manger in Bethlehem cradled a king who would be unheralded by most of his own subjects, even though his kingship knew no bounds. The hymn writer captures the paradox with the words, "O Jesus the crucified! Thee will I sing, my blessed Redeemer, my God and my King."[5] The Crucified and the Creator were somehow a single, marvelous, personal, redemptive reality.

The Christmas story is arranged like a musical score, with its treble and bass clefs needing to be read simultaneously. On the bass clef are the usual human events, a crowded little town, more taxes than the people can bear, a shortage of accommodations, the resulting suffering of the financially weak, the pain of childbirth, the rumors, and the arrogant use of political power to eliminate competition for the throne. This is the low of the world. On the treble clef is a secret in Mary's heart, angels singing in heaven, and a generally unrecognized divine intervention into this sordid stream of human affairs. O little town of Bethlehem, how burdened and how blessed! The treble and bass clefs of this Christmas score must be harmonized by the eyes of faith or the whole truth will never be known about Jesus or God. Take them together or take them not at all. A little human baby had been born; God had come to be with us so that we might be with God. A human cry came out of a crude cradle; the loving heart of God was breaking under the weight of your sin and mine. The cry and the heart were one.

The Gospel of Mark is an excellent example of how Christians from the beginning have seen in Jesus a divine "incarnation," God joining humanity through the life of a real man. Mark gives a human picture of Jesus, "the carpenter" (6:3), driven into the wilderness to be tempted (1:12), a man of deep human emotions, plagued on occasion by hunger and tiredness, ignited on occasion to righteous anger. But Mark never neglects a controlling belief: "The beginning of the gospel of Jesus Christ, the *Son of God*" (1:1). People had been astonished at the words and deeds of this Jesus. His closest friends were filled with awe and said to each other, "Who then is this, that even the wind and sea obey him?" (4:41). To Mark, Jesus was not simply a man among men. Somehow, the full truth was that Jesus was *God among men*. He was the final fulfillment of what humans should be and the final revelation of what God always has been.

There you have the paradox, the first two elements of the Christian understanding of the one God. In Christ, a completely human nature and the nature of God were united, without a reduction of either the humanity or the divinity. It was a necessary paradox that arose from the life experience of those early believers and inevitably worked its way into the development of the formal doctrines of the church. Those first disciples knew Jesus to be a real man. Nonetheless, in his presence they found themselves confronting God. Jesus' life was recognized to be nothing less than the life of God active in history on their behalf. So much was this the case that those first believers could no longer think of God without first thinking of Jesus. After all, it was in Jesus that they had met God most directly, understandably, and savingly. There are not multiple gods, of course; there is one God who is made present and known in Jesus Christ. The whole truth is in the confluence of these two truths.

Such knowledge of God came through the teachings, compassion, and sacrifice of Jesus. It was confirmed by the sheer quality of his life and sealed forever by the events surrounding his death. In fact, the resurrection of Jesus from the dead became the pivotal event that caused intense reflection on the question of who Jesus really was. The disciples only came to understand the full implications of the Christmas events as they saw them from the later vantage-point of the Easter events. What these disciples came to understand through what Jesus had said and done was that *God* had spoken, that God is a loving Father, and that God in Jesus Christ had given freely of himself for the sake of their salvation. To begin with Jesus is the best way to end with God.

Both High and Nigh

The biblically revealed God is both mighty and merciful, standing high above all creation, while also being intimately involved in the creation's life.

The biblical story highlights the paradoxical view that God is both *high* and *nigh*. On the one hand, Jewish tradition taught that God is "high and lifted up," the distant Creator whose name must be held in great reverence. Such an emphasis was effective in avoiding idolatry and keeping men and women from thinking of God merely in terms of themselves. Human thoughts and ways are not those of God.

This intense reverence, however, often resulted in lifting God out of the intimate secrets and personal needs of everyday people. In the Jewish national consciousness, God kept slipping from being their savior at the Exodus and comforter during the Exile to being little more than an accepted theological axiom that held together their religious traditions. God meant all to them, but often they held God so high in the sky and so distant in their memories that Yahweh became impersonal and virtually lost in abstraction. Those Jews with little historical interest or theological commitment came to this natural conclusion. If God is effectively removed from an active relationship with the things that concerned them most, then God really did not concern them at all.

According to Christian belief, the *high* of God became clearer to humans as the *nigh* of God when God breeched the divine-human gap by coming *in person*. God felt our pains and healed our dreaded diseases, coming as the Almighty One, but in the form of a servant. He came in Jesus Christ to identify with us, be self-revealed to us, and be near us in an unexpectedly humble and fatherly way. God gave himself sacrificially. He invited weary humans to drink in divine love and be cleansed by divine forgiveness. From so far, God came so near. On the cross of Jesus and in the mouth of that empty tomb, those lovely, paradoxical words came true, "So great, so pure, so high...and who is always nigh."[6]

The Gospel of Mark includes the story of an obscure woman who made only a momentary appearance in the public eye. By usual standards, she was only a statistic. She came up behind Jesus in a shoving crowd and touched his garment in a daring act of faith. She is an unknown person except for that brief moment when she commanded the undivided attention of Jesus. He who was with God at the creation of the world chose to enter the lonely and desperate struggle of this unidentified woman. The lights went down on that surging crowd until it seemed that Jesus and the woman were all alone. They exchanged words, and the adequacy of his caring penetrated her deepest need. She was whole again. She had touched Jesus, and God had touched her. The Almighty who dwells far above the mundane of this world was also right where she needed him to be, close to a nameless woman in the midst of a surging crowd.

The prayer that Jesus taught his disciples to pray begins by addressing God with the very personal "Our Father." How easy it has been over the centuries to cheapen this phrase, so that it becomes an excuse for a comfortable and irresponsible religion. God has come to be seen as so daddy-like, personal and near, so sympathetic and forgiving that one can almost presume on the divine. In the same way, many think of Jesus as a meek young man, dressed in a white sheet, typically found playing with lambs and joking with children. Such people have fallen prey to the sin of sentimentalizing. They are so impressed with the closeness and gentleness of God in Jesus that the divine distance, majesty, and judgment are largely forgotten. The high-nigh paradox must remain in tact.

Christians have attracted considerable criticism from skeptics who have seen the church as a collection of weak persons reaching for security in troubled times. God, so the critics have argued, has been manufactured in credulous minds so that there might be an available alternative to all of the limitations and anxieties of struggling humanity. God has been only a mirage of our own making. To such skeptics, believing is the ultimate, understandable, but empty act of our human helplessness.

As so often happens, an adequate response to such criticism must begin by recognizing that there is some truth to the charge! We are weak and anxious people searching for salvation and security. The loving God made known in Jesus Christ does provide answers and resources for survival. Even so, at least as witnessed to in the Judaeo-Christian tradition, God has little if anything to do with a bellhop deity who rushes to fulfill all human desires. To the contrary, from the day that God first commanded Abraham to leave the security of his city for the dangers and unknowns of the desert, the God of biblical revelation has given no excuse for settling down in material comfort and spiritual complacency. God, as self-revealed, is a demanding, empowering, and commissioning God, a restless force always leading people into the new and unknown. God lives more in tents than in temples.

We contemporary Christians must resurrect "Our Father" from this persistent confusion. God is loving and forgiving, near and available to needy men and women. But this does not eliminate an equal and coordinate truth. That model prayer of Jesus goes on to say, "Our Father *who art in heaven.*" The Jews resisted vigorously the danger of sentimentalizing the love of God and slipping into a subtle idolatry. God is both loving and holy, twin truths we must remain caught between. Since God is God, we must know and relate by loving in response to divine love and by reverencing God in light of his sovereignty and holiness. By God's grace, we may commune with the very heart of the divine. But, by the nature of things, we also must commune by carefully mixing repentance, responsibility, love, awe, reverence, and worship.

Those early disciples of Jesus learned that God is both *merciful* and *mighty*. Here are two adjectives that do not normally go together. People have been tormented over the centuries by persons of power who arbitrarily use that power against other persons. It has become everyday knowledge that power tends to corrupt, and that absolute power has a way of corrupting absolutely. When power has been raised to the level of the divine, people have trembled in utter fear of its fickle and vindictive use. They have done everything imaginable to appease gods who were thought to be both angry and fully capable of venting their anger on helpless humans. Even the Old Testament mentions times when the God of Israel is said to have slashed out in anger and taken revenge on enemies and punished the faithlessness of his own people. Absolute power is assumed to be a fearsome thing, especially if the possessor of such power is not fully known and trusted.

The questions, then, are basic. Are there any self-limitations that God has imposed on the use of divine power, any restrictions beyond which God *can* but typically chooses *not* to go? Is there some cosmic context in which the employing of divine capacities is consistently controlled? If God is almighty, is God also malignant, capricious, and uncaring? How is God related to disastrous floods, killing famines, dying saints, or the fate of those who openly oppose God's will and yet seem to do very well in this world?

What should one make of the witness of the famous Christian hymn writer, Fanny J. Crosby? Apparently, when an infant, a stranger treated her eye inflammation with "hot poultices"—a treatment that rendered Fanny blind for life. In fact, as it turned out, her blindness opened some doors for her later ministry that would not have been open otherwise. Crosby said that her Christian faith had provided her with the assurance that this stranger had been an instrument in God's hands to "consecrate" her to her life's work. She recalled her mother having instilled in her the view that "sometimes Providence deprived persons of some physical faculty in order that the spiritual insight might more fully awaken."[7] Does God blind some children and take others prematurely in death, all for a higher good that we cannot understand?

As always, two things must be said. First, the God made known by the life, death, and resurrection of our Lord Jesus Christ is infinite in all ways that are consistent with the divine character. Being rational, God is capable of all rational pursuits. Being personal, God's rational thoughts and actions involve a consciously sensitive being who is aware of the network of personal relationships involved in any action. Most importantly, as understood through Christ, this loving God is merciful as well as mighty. Unlimited rational and personal capacities are tempered by an amazing love that was dramatically demonstrated in the sacrifice of Jesus. "Holy, holy, holy," exclaims our hymnal, "merciful and mighty...perfect in power, in love and purity."[8]

Such a loving God, as understood most fully through Jesus Christ, obviously has imposed "self-limitations" (voluntarily, of course, since there is nothing external to God capable of imposing limitations). Biblical revelation makes clear that God both affects the world and is affected by it. Jesus taught us that one cannot really love without becoming vulnerable to the object of one's love. In the original creation, God chose to take a "risk" by lovingly granting some measure of freedom to the creation. The Bible reveals God as a dynamic personal agent who, by sovereign choice, is vulnerably involved in human joys and sorrows, sins and salvation. Christian theology often speaks more of God's power than of divine "weakness," more of eternal majesty than temporal engagement. Even so, the key fact of Christian faith is that the Word became *flesh*, a dramatic statement of God's relational engagement and changing unchangeability! In the paradox of this changing and unchanging lies the pulsating heart of biblical revelation, which includes both the sovereign God who stands *above* creation and the compassionate God who stoops to significant involvement *with* the creation.

A balance must be reached between the "opposing" truths of God's absolute sovereignty and the world's relative independence from that sovereignty. The meaningfulness of intercessory prayer, for instance, depends on whether God sometimes wills to respond to individual human petitions in the midst of what seems to be an autonomous and impersonal world. It is clear that, on the one hand, we live in a world of real contingencies, genuine tragedies, and hateful relationships that injure innocent and often God-fearing people. All of this happens within the general oversight of an almighty and loving God. On the other hand, there is the undeniable biblical witness to special moments when God chooses to intervene, when divine compassion or anger thrusts itself into a situation more decisively than at other times. Both emphases are true, while neither is fully true apart from the other.

We humans seldom analyze successfully and never dictate the activity or seeming passivity of God; but we can hold steady and not rush to one extreme or the other in our judgments. We learn best by what appear to be divine actions, despite our continuing inability to see God directly. As one stanza of Christina Rossetti's poem "Who Has Seen the Wind" pictures the circumstance by analogy:

> Who has seen the wind?
>   Neither you nor I:
> But when the trees bow down their heads,
>   The wind is passing by.

The paradox is that we learn to observe meaningfully the essentially unobservable.

Those early disciples learned through Jesus Christ that God is both *loving* and *just*. God is not that sentimental grandfather in the sky who is able to look past all wrong and freely forgive all things without pain and high cost. Nor is God that stern judge at every turn of life who sees evil and distributes punishments without hesitation or exception. God is, in one sense, both of these, and in the highest sense neither. God is just and does condemn what is unholy. There are consequences to be faced. And yet, God also would rather console than condemn, overtaking the lost with the warmth of forgiveness and bringing them home to the loving heart of the divine. God is both high and nigh, unlimited in capacity and also abounding in compassion.

The Beauty of the Ugly Cross

*One disgraceful and very ugly death somehow has become
the door to a grace-provided and unspeakably beautiful life
for all who will believe.*

Divine justice and love somehow appeared simultaneously at the cross of Jesus. Here was the timeless test case, that ultimate moment when people were privileged to peer most deeply into the very heart of God. Would the divine love for humans go to this length of complete divine humiliation? Would justice be satisfied if Christ's blood were shed? Could an apparent tragedy such as the cruelty of the cross be the seedbed for atonement, a renewed at-one-ment between God and sinners? Unexplainably, but definitely, and irreversibly, the answers are all "Yes!" Somehow that gruesome event on Golgotha was the necessary sign of God's love and the necessary satisfaction of God's requirements of justice. Jesus had revealed the very heart of a loving Father. He also had, through the giving of himself, cleared all unpayable accounts. The cross became the crucial means of divine revelation and an adequate vehicle of human redemption.

The meaning of the death of Jesus goes beyond somehow being the means of eternal salvation. It also is the ultimate expression of God's way to life for us who believe. Paradoxically, the cross is death, and yet it is the way to the only real life. Here are key truths to be caught between. Life is found by losing it, just as a grain of wheat must die in order to yield its fruit (Jn. 12:24f). At the cross, the "mind" of Christ was seen in his utter self-giving, the very mind that ought to be in us (Phil. 2:5 ff). Jesus' death revealed the nature of the way; his resurrection demonstrated the power and ultimate victory of the way. The cross alone "would show us how to die in order to live, but the resurrection enables us to die the death that leads to life."[9] It also shows us the proper way to think about God.

Cross-like thinking about God leads to the very heart of biblical revelation. One theologian speaks of the "cruciform church."[10] Church life should be cross-like. Likewise, we should think as follows about the dominating motivation most characteristic of divine sovereignty. It should be more the motive of *love* than the maintenance of *full control*. Here is the beautiful paradox of divine sovereignty: "Suffering is not inherent in God, but God freely wills to enter into our suffering so that it can be overcome. God cannot be changed by either heavenly or earthly powers, but God can change himself. He remains unchanging in his will for the world, but he alters his ways with his people in conjunction with their response to his gracious initiative. God enters into a reciprocal relationship with his people so that we can have a role in the realization of his plan and purpose."[11] God chooses to suffer in order that we can choose to live!

The cross of Christ is a prime example of the mystery of Christian faith. Nothing is more central, no event more clearly recorded, no truth more profoundly paradoxical. About one-fourth of the material in the four Gospels is concerned with the cross. This mass of material seeks to recount historically how the death of Jesus came about, what it means theologically, and how it was an ugly death leading to a beautiful life. Even so, the death of Jesus is so profound an event that no one definition, no one concept of it can fully capture its significance for our salvation or the means by which it becomes significant in our behalf. It was a marvelous reality, but a marvel wrapped in mystery.

In fact, the New Testament sets forth the significance of the cross of Jesus with a rich variety of terms and analogies. The final significance is never completely captured by any one apart from the others. Fortunately, the power of the cross is not kept from us until we can fully comprehend its meaning! Christ defeated the devil, absorbed evil and made it the raw material for good, freed humans from the fear of death (Heb. 2:14), completed the long process of human restoration after the Fall, saying "It is finished!" (Jn. 19:30), gave his life a ransom for many (Mark 10:45), paid the price of human sin (it is not clear to whom he made the payment—he just paid it all), laid bare before us the loving heart of the eternal Father (2 Cor. 4:6), and became a sacrificial lamb (Heb. 5:9, 7:27, 10:11-12). The images and explanations are several. They are all meaningful, and all incomplete. We are caught among them, instructed by them, committed to all of them—and to none of them apart from the others. The divine fact transcends our fumbling attempts at explanation.

What Paul did in his writings was to take from the ordinary life of his day several common scenes and use them as metaphors for exposing the profound mystery of what was accomplished by the cross of Jesus. According to these metaphors, we have been justified as a defendant vindicated in a court of law, reconciled as two friends who had been separated, redeemed as God had earlier brought the Jews out of Egypt or as a Greek slave might buy freedom, adopted as an orphaned child, and atoned since the necessary price is now fully paid.

There is foundational truth in all of these metaphors, even though there is adequacy in no single one to ever fully "explain" the exact meaning of the cross. The only adequacy available is not in our attempts at explanation, but in the person of Christ and in the overriding truth. That truth is that Jesus did die and rise again by the power of God and *on our behalf*. The death and resurrection of Jesus clarify for us the unlimited power and forgiving love of God. They clear the way for us to regain our lost stature as sons and daughters of the heavenly Father.

With this clarifying and amazing bottom line in mind, we should be aware of the inadequacy of common language and simple logic to capture full meaning when it comes to God. The nature of God and of God's gracious work on our behalf are profound realities. We cannot understand adequately the full meaning of the cross of Christ. We can only stand in silence before it, acknowledge its wonder, and submit to its gracious power. The humble Christian should be led "to the language of worship, a language less precise, though more profound and thus more adequate than rational formulas and arid arguments. Standing before God inspires song more readily than academic dissertations."[12]

The Departed Is Still With Us!

The grace of the Lord Jesus Christ was really the grace of God who was one with Christ in his life, death, and resurrection. According to the doctrine of the Trinity, there then comes the "communion of the Holy Spirit." This three-part story of the one God moves from the sovereign God, who becomes known through a servant Son, to a continuous ministry of divine revelation and redemption through the Spirit. The paradox of this tri-unity expands further since placing them in time sequence is for narrative convenience only. After all, it was the Spirit who brooded over the water of the first creation (Gen. 1) and the Son who was one with the Father even before the creation (Jn. 1:3). Our saying first the Father, then the Son, and finally the Spirit is merely a reflection of how we tell the story of God with us—the triune God who always is one living, saving, and present reality.

What makes this good-news drama of divine incarnation in Jesus surpass the mysteries of fiction and the careers of other historical figures is not the way it ends (the suspense build-up of most fiction). The stunning fact of this divine drama is that *it has not yet ended*. This Jesus, this itinerant preacher from Galilee, killed at the height of a Jewish Passover celebration, has been more alive after his death than before. In fact, the life story of Jesus the Christ is still in process, with no end in sight. The central paradox of his being the God-Man is paralleled only by the stunning fact that he was successfully executed and still refuses to die! In him, death always yields to life. God is the ever-living One who accepts death into his own grieving heart so that the sin of the creation can be atoned and its true life restored. The One who once died is life itself.

The Holy Spirit is none other than the Spirit of Christ, an extension of the life and ministry of Jesus, functioning in the present, primarily as a witness to Christ (Jn. 15:26; 16:13-15). The Gospels make it clear that, up to the point of the crucifixion of their Lord, the disciples were faltering in their understanding of Jesus' teachings. But after the resurrection they came to understand much more fully. They were taught by the light of dramatic events and by virtue of the Spirit's leading. Jesus had told them to expect that the Spirit would "teach you all things, and bring to your remembrance all that I said to you" (Jn. 14:26). In every age, the Spirit, God remaining with us, testifies to believing hearts about Christ, that is, about the God in Jesus who was, is, and ever shall be, one God without beginning or ending. This witnessing Spirit is the continuing presence of Jesus Christ (Jn. 20:22). Paul could actually write of the risen Christ and the Holy Spirit in a way that makes their identities almost interchangeable (Rom. 8:9 f).

At this point we must exercise great caution. Nothing is easier than to exalt the universal Spirit of Christ, who is above the limitations of time and place, at the expense of the historical event of Jesus, who was limited by time and place. If we say Father and Spirit, de-emphasizing the Son, we lose the anchorage of the historical revelation that defines the Father and provides the substance of the Spirit's witness. It is vital that we have a personal encounter with the living Christ here and now. But such subjective communion must not drift away from its moorings in the event of the defining reality who lived long ago. The divine coming to us now is an extension of God's incarnate coming then. Although common practice in recent centuries, it is fatal to New Testament faith either to separate Jesus from the present, confining him to the "primitive" setting of the first century. We must not uproot the "contemporary Christ" from the recorded events of first-century Palestine. The past-present paradox must remain whole. The ministry of the Spirit is the linkage.

The Three-One God

*God being both three and one may not be great math,
but it is orthodox Christian theology.*

The magazine *People* did a special story on Lawrence Spivak as he was about to retire from thirty years of hosting the popular radio and television program *Meet The Press*. Spivak recounted how President John F. Kennedy had been opposed to his younger brother "Teddy" voluntarily subjecting himself to the television cameras and questions. "You've got nothing to gain and a lot to lose," he had argued. But Teddy went ahead and even tried to handle a tough question on the issue of church and state. President Kennedy called Spivak the next day to see what Spivak thought of Teddy's answer to that most politically explosive issue. Spivak admitted that he had not "the slightest idea what Teddy was talking about. It was such a confusing answer." Then the President said, "Yeah, wasn't that good?"[13] Deliberate ambiguity is good politics; but is it necessary or tolerable in Christian theology?

In Christian theology, key paradoxes are not strategic evasions, deliberate complications to mask the plain truth. Rather, they are required by the nature of the truth itself. Since this is the case, I offer one final reminder in the face of many accusations that defining God as "the great three-in-one" is a meaningless riddle left over from the church's dogma developed centuries ago. The fact is that there is no "orthodox" choice but to stay with this complexity. "Trinity," when speaking of the one God, is not a way of hiding or confusing the truth. It is the only adequate way of pointing to the full profundity of the truth itself. The Christian faith centers its belief in the *one* God who, as biblically revealed, is somehow *three*! Here is wisdom:

> In order to avoid tri-theism [three gods], we say that the Trinity is a society of persons united by a common divinity. There is one God, eternal, uncreated, incomprehensible, and there is no other. But God's nature is internally complex and consists of a fellowship of three. It is the essence of God's nature to be relational. This is primordial in God and defines who God is. God is a triadic community, not a single, undifferentiated unity.[14]

The doctrine of the Trinity, while uncomfortable in its inherent awkwardness (one God being three), is nonetheless essential. It is not a deliberate evasion of the task of dealing straightforwardly with a central theological issue. Even less is it mere church tradition or theological double-talk. Rather than an abstract mathematical formula, it is a summary description of the Bible's view of God as eternal love, incarnate in Jesus Christ, through the ever-present Spirit.

The New Testament knows God as Father, Son, and Holy Spirit, while it also knows God as one alone. In God's transcendence we have the Father; in God's immanence we have the Spirit; and in God's ultimate historical disclosure we are blessed to have the Son. God is all of these or God is less than has been revealed in the New Testament. There is no way to the *one* except by way of these *three*. To say "God" as Christians, we are obliged, by the instruction of divine revelation, to say three words, else we have stopped short of the larger truth. The "Trinity" is the church's faltering attempt to recount with adequacy who God is through how God has become known to us humans.

Not only must we say Father, Son, and Spirit in order to say all that should be said. We must act in light of all three. There are those who love Jesus as an historical model for their lives, but have no sense of the eternal Father, and seemingly have not even heard of the baptism of the Spirit that could empower their very existence. There are whole congregations whose public experiences of worship refer reverently to the Father and relate in a very orthodox fashion to the true identity of the Son, but seem to lack the Holy Spirit's gifting and power. It is much like showing appropriate respect for the antiques of another age. The church must remember the past, to be sure, but it must be more than a museum of orthodox traditions and doctrines. The reverse is also true. There are those groups of Christians who so constantly indulge in the raptures of the Holy Spirit's presence that they become self-absorbed in their own experiences. They lose the sense of divine sovereignty and fail to follow through by actually doing Christ's will in the world.

The doctrine of the Trinity is the shoreline that ought to mark the limits of our thinking about God and our acting in light of God. Here is an excellent summary statement:

> He is the God who from the beginning has been calling man into a covenant relation with himself, in which alone life in this world makes sense and has a future. When his call from beyond our world was insufficient, he came to us in a person of our own flesh and blood and in him knocked on the door of our human life. He came in search of us in Jesus Christ and, where men let themselves be found, he took possession of their very selves, indwelt them with his Spirit, and through them extended his search for man. The Trinity describes God's invasion of our world, and the question for us is how we shall respond to this invader. Faith in him is surrender to his invasion, openness to the life he brings, readiness to let the life that comes to us from him go on through us to others.[15]

Isaiah includes a classic passage that recounts vividly his personal experience of God's immediate presence. Overwhelmed by God's holiness, Isaiah opened his life, sensed his own sin, and yielded both to the lure of a loving forgiveness and to the vision of a divine mission. Later, he tried to describe the scene and its results (Isa. 6). Note that Isaiah does not describe God in any direct way. The description is limited to the train that filled the temple, the angels that surrounded the throne, the shaking of the foundations, and the smoke that filled the house. In this way, Isaiah indicates two important truths that constitute a pivotal paradox.

The *revelation* of God is, at the same time, a *veiling* of God. God, mysteriously, necessarily, mercifully, remains hidden, even when in the process of self-revealing. We may learn God's name, or see God's shadow, or hear God's voice, but somehow God always stands above and beyond our sight. We see God by grace, although no human eye has ever seen. We know God by grace, although the fullness of the divine is always beyond our knowing. We are caught in the paradox of *knowing-unknowing*. Thus, we have knowledge of the divine without ourselves being or becoming divine. While we truly are visited by God, our humility is always mandated in the face of divinity. We cannot adequately label or physically seize, never fully comprehend or selfishly control God. What we can do is approach and appreciate, contact and be converted by the great Sovereign who, by the agency of the Son and the Spirit's ministry, has come near and clear, all without becoming restricted to the limits of our experience or the frailties of our understanding.

Paul's greeting to the Corinthians was that "the grace of the Lord Jesus Christ, and the love of God, and the communion of the Holy Spirit, be with you all!" (2 Cor. 13:14). Although ministers have adapted these words for use as a benediction at the end of sermons and services, they are equally proper as an invocation or as a concise summary of basic Christian assumptions. The Creator God, in diverse ways throughout all time, has been seeking fallen humans in love. May we permit ourselves to be found!

Notes

1. Clark H. Pinnock, *Most Moved Mover* (Grand Rapids: Baker Academic, 2001), 30.

2. Martin Marty, *Martin Luther* (Viking Penguin, 2004), 10.

3. Albert Schweitzer, *The Quest of the Historical Jesus* (London: Adam & Charles Black, 1910), 401.

4. D. M. Baillie, *God Was In Christ* (New York: Charles Scribner's Sons, 1948), 64.

5. Hymn, "O Sing of His Mighty Love" (verse 4), by Frank Bottome and William B. Bradbury.

6. Hymn, "None Is Like God" (verse 1), by John Burton and John B. Dykes.

7. Edith L. Blumhofer, *Her Heart Can See: The Life and Hymns of Fanny J. Crosby* (Grand Rapids: Eerdmans, 2005), 15-16.

8. Hymn, "Holy, Holy, Holy! Lord God Almighty" (verses 1 and 3), by Reginald Heber and John B. Dykes.

9. Frank Stagg, *New Testament Theology* (Nashville: Broadman Press, 1962), 123.

10. C. Leonard Allen, *The Cruciform Church: Becoming a Cross-Shaped People in a Secular World* (Abilene, Texas: Abilene Christian University Press, 1990).

11. Donald Bloesch, *God the Almighty* (Downers Grove, Ill.: InterVarsity Press, 1995), 95.

12. Barry L. Callen, *God As Loving Grace* (Nappanee, Ind.: Evangel Publishing House, 1996), 252.

13. In the periodical *People* (August, 1975).

14. Clark H. Pinnock, in *Flame of Love*, as quoted in Barry L. Callen, *Discerning the Divine* (Louisville: Westminster John Knox Press, 2004), 171.

15. James D. Smart, *The ABC's of Christian Faith* (Philadelphia: The Westminster Press, 1968), 43.

Humans—Crown and Crisis of Creation

Man, a nothing in comparison with the Infinite, and All in comparison with the Nothing, a mean between nothing and everything.
—Pascal

The talk of mankind come of age is sheer cant; we are actually closer to the kindergarten.... The Christian faith, whatever else it may be, is not sentimental; it does not speak of the inevitability of progress or of "men like gods." Whenever it is loyal to Christ, it stresses both elements in the paradox of the nobility and degradation of mankind.[1]

God has come to us self-revealingly in Jesus Christ, and God's gracious and redeeming presence still remains with us in the ministry of the Holy Spirit. Therefore, we humans have valuable perspective on the real nature of ourselves as persons in this world. There is a place to start in our search for understanding our many problems as we struggle with the troubling realities so obvious in this world and in ourselves.

What do we know? We know at least that God is available to help define properly the real problems of life and make possible genuine solutions. As the two quotes above make clear, we need to be sensitive to the paradoxical reality of humankind. There should be no sliding into shallow sentimentality by a missing of the *degradation* of humans; nor should there be any premature despair by a missing of the *nobility* of humans. We are caught between these twin realities.

Two Diverging Roads

*Humans know a severe dividedness within themselves.
We are half dust and half deity.*

The poet Robert Frost once pictured two roads diverging and then disappearing into a heavily wooded area. He suggested the potential importance of choosing the road least traveled.[2] Similarly, when we try to identify our own nature as men and women, we come to this image of the two roads. We observe that, as human beings, we are particularly blessed by God's original creation and continuing presence. But it is also evident that we are cursed by a dividedness in our own nature that is both brightened by divine light and overshadowed by a dark evil. We cannot avoid being torn by the hard choices of life that are always before us—and we know that the choices will make all the difference! Ironically, we seem destined to go both ways at the same time. Something within our very nature pulls toward the good; something else persists in pulling the other way.

Fedor Dostoevsky projected into his fictional characters a deep doubleness that he had first discovered in himself. He knew himself to be a man who was both vain and humble, demanding and self-sacrificing, irritable and devoted. In a similar way, Lord Byron, that club-footed English romantic who led a sordid personal life, once commented that humans are "half dust, half deity, alike unfit to sink or soar."

Who are we anyway? Milton Berle, a comedian who brought such laughter and relaxation to millions of Americans for decades, admitted in his autobiography that his life ran "on guilt and adrenalin."[3] His humor was haunted by the less than funny. How typical this seems to be! It is the old problem stated by the Paul in Romans, chapter seven. There was an inner war in progress within Paul, a war being fought over his own willingness and ability to take that road least used and thereby to do with joy the known will of God. He knew the good and wanted to do it, and yet leaned distressingly toward the bad. Paul's resulting cry is so understandable: "Wretched man that I am! Who will rescue me from this body of death?" (Rom. 7:24).

Many of the papers of Dietrich Bonhoeffer have survived his Nazi imprisonment in the 1940s. A particularly insightful piece is titled "Who Am I?" This persecuted and lonely Christian man poured out his feelings of remorse, assurance, doubt, and faith. He questioned...

> Am I then really all that which other men tell of? Or am I only what I myself know of myself?... Am I one person today and tomorrow another? Am I both at once? A hypocrite before others, and before myself a contemptibly woebegone weakling?... Whoever I am, Thou knowest, O God, I am Thine![4]

These intimate words of Bonhoeffer reflect the doubleness that plagues our human existence. Just who are we? Do we mislead others with multiple masks? Do we even know? Psalm 82:6 says that we are "gods"—

and this passage is quoted approvingly by Jesus in John 10:34. But Isaiah 40:6-7 says that we are "grass"—and this passage is quoted approvingly in 1 Peter 1:24-25. Are we gods or grass? Or are we both? Yes, we are. We are caught between these twin truths of human existence. We are persons of paradox.

Jesus explains in John 10:35 that we are "gods" because the Word of God has come to us and we have the spiritual capacity to receive and be renewed by it. Isaiah emphasizes the theme of humans as withering "grass" because of the obvious brevity and frailty of our lives. Both insights are true, leaving us to understand ourselves as composite beings, persons of the highest capacities who, nonetheless, are hanging only by a thread. We are both-and beings caught in the midst of conflicting realities lodged in our own nature.

The whole truth of our situation must come to terms with a deep fissure in the very nature of the cosmos, a gulf that separates good and evil, the spiritually whole and the seriously fallen, life and death. Most of us have two feet as part of our human bodies. What is more significant and less obvious is that, as part of the very essence of our beings, we seem at once to have a foot placed in each of two different worlds. We complex grass-god beings straddle a deep gorge of existence, with one foot on either edge of opposing cliffs. It is precisely because we are partly on one side that we need salvation; and it is precisely because we are partly on the other side that we are capable of being saved. We are both the *crown* and the *crisis* of God's creation.

If we look at this dualism politically, we could say with Reinhold Niebuhr that "man's capacity for justice makes democracy *possible*; but man's inclination to injustice makes democracy *necessary*."[5] If we see this doubleness from a theological viewpoint, we view ourselves as created beings wholly dependent on God for our existence. But we also see that we are in a *middle state*, for we have been given a share in the creating activity of God. Created humans are empowered to be creators, co-workers with God in shaping the very creation of which we are a part and for which we share responsibility. Further, this middle state is a sadly *mixed* state since we who are called to work *with* God often choose to work *against* God's purposes in this world.

Humans, paradoxical creatures of the dust. Humans, creations of God and constant objects of God's love. Humans, the reason for the ultimate sacrifice of Jesus on that rugged Roman cross. Humans, companions of God in the garden of bliss and aggressors who, at the crucifixion of Jesus, were seen with the weapons of defiance in their hands.

Humans, suspended between life and death, good and evil, hope and despair. Humans—me, you! We are simultaneously the apex and low-point of creation. God loves, wills love, and also provides the freedom to humans that opens the door both to the highest of divine-human relationships and the lowest of human evils. Any assessment that fails to take into account the whole of this paradox is seriously inadequate.

Both Flesh and Spirit

Despite the consequences of the sin and fallenness of the world, the creation remains the domain of God and is capable of holiness.[6]

Note the following lines from a contemporary poem that sets the scene of the human dilemma in a graphic way. Explaining that late afternoon was his best time to write, a poet reports:

> Then I remove my clothes and leave them in a pile
> as if I had melted to death and my legacy consisted of only
> a white shirt, a pair of pants, and a pot of cold tea.
>
> Then I remove my flesh and hang it over a chair.
> I slide it off my bones like a silken garment.
> I do this so that what I write will be pure,
> completely rinsed of the carnal,
> uncontaminated by the preoccupations of the body.[7]

The poet's reasoning may reflect an admirable attempt at self-cleansing, but it raises central theological questions. The flesh certainly can be "distracting," but is it "carnal" in the sense of being inherently evil, and thus the enemy of "purity" in writing and living? Much ancient thought that influenced early and even recent Christian thinking answers "yes." However, the Bible suggests repeatedly that the flesh is *not* inherently evil. It was God who originally hung our flesh "like a silken garment" over our bones and said that it was *good* (Gen. 1:31).

There is a tragic irony at the root of our human dilemma. According to the biblical story, our bondage is self-inflicted. It is the result of a frantic attempt on our part to be free, free even from the God who created and granted the freedom that enables our potential rebellion and ruin. For some tragic reason, we have turned our own way in self-love, self-assertion, and self-destruction. Wanting to be sovereign apart from God, we have become enslaved to sin and death. Our awkward thrust toward an unnatural freedom has forced us into an unwanted slavery. From a biblical perspective, we humans have been affected deeply by this deliberate distortion of ourselves. It is called "sin" and "evil," which is "live" spelled backwards. We have reversed how things ought to be, with tragic results.

Humans are viewed variously in the Bible as flesh (*sarx*), spirit (*pneuma*), body (*soma*), and soul (*psuche*). In each instance, however, humans are viewed as a *whole*, as a total human person who is being considered at various times from the perspective of only one of these dimensions of our single complexity. We humans are not, for instance, bodies *and* souls. We are body-souls, bodies with a spiritual dimension and spirits with a physical existence. To see ourselves as one of these to the exclusion of the other is to invite real confusion. For instance, to assume that we are immortal as "soul" and mortal as "body" is false theology—humans are *not* inherently immortal. To assume that one aspect of ourselves is evil while another is good is also misleading and not the approach of the Bible to the nature of the human being. Much in the history of Christian spirituality has sought to control, even beat and starve the physical body, thinking that it is the source of evil. This has been wrong.

Because so much Christian thought has been influenced by Greek philosophic concepts, some important clarity is required. For the ancient Greek, the flesh of the human body is the evil prison-house of the soul. In fact, the whole material universe is judged to be evil, with spirit alone thought to be good. Such an assumption can have drastic consequences as we engage in self-evaluation and choose a course of action in life—particularly regarding subjects like sexuality, politics, and ecology. It is crucial to note that the Hebrew (biblical) tradition differs sharply from this Greek approach, even though some of Paul's statements in the New Testament, when taken in isolation, do not always reflect the difference clearly.

Paul states in 2 Corinthians 10:3: "For though we walk in the flesh, we do not war according to the flesh" (NASB). In this one verse, Paul is using the word "flesh" in two different ways. To walk *in the flesh* (NRSV says "live as human beings") is something we all must do—that is the material substance of our existence. To war *according to the flesh* (NRSV says "according to human standards") is an optional activity that we are being called to avoid. The first reference to "flesh" is neutral; the second is laden with negative overtones. According to Paul's thought, when the "old man is crucified with Christ," when we have passed from the old to the new life, we are still in the flesh, but no longer "after the flesh." The Spirit of Christ abides in us so that we come to walk *according to the Spirit*. "The life which I now live in the flesh," says Paul, "I live by faith in the Son of God" (Gal. 2:20).

The very same instincts, passions, and emotions that were the raw material of sin apparently can come under the control of Christ and be transformed into building blocks of righteousness. The exercise of our sexuality, for instance, can be the best or worst of human relationships. Our bodies are not to be detested, but fully utilized, even enjoyed. When they are channeled by God's enabling Spirit toward the divinely established functions and ultimate goals of human life, they are "saved," "redeemed," restored to their original intention.

Paul, seeing the warfare in humans, said that the conflict was between two opposing forces, "flesh" and "spirit" (Gal. 5:17). What is the reason for this warfare? While the ancient Greek world tended to see the evil residing in our physical existence as humans, Paul's New Testament writings go another way. They insist that our mortal bodies can become alive with the very life of Christ—thus, they are not inherently evil. "Sarx" (fleshly existence) is more than a biblical reference to our physical bodies; it sometimes means "human nature as it has become through sin."[8] That nature is redeemable through divine grace.

We humans are a singularity, but not a simple singularity. A multi-dimensional approach is always warranted, even though the basic wholeness must be kept in view. We are yes-and-no beings. There are three interactive insights into human nature found in the Bible. No one of these is rightly understood unless it is seen in light of the other two. It is important to review each briefly, and consciously relate each to the others. To not have the *whole* picture is to see the *wrong* picture. To separate parts from the whole is to create a lie with pieces of the truth.

1. Humans are made in the image of God.

We are unique in all creation. We are able to respond to God's gracious availability and thus become responsible for God's gracious offers and expectations. We are free—not altogether, but enough to make us fully responsible. We are rational, moral beings, fashioned for fulfillment, commissioned to subdue, organize, and be the faithful stewards of all other elements of creation. We are the crown of God's creation, even intended co-creators with God as the divine purpose moves on through time.

God initiated the creation and judged it essentially "good." We humans are designed to be reflections of God's highest intent in creation. We have been granted a dignity, an ultimate worth that demands constant respect. The Bible warns that, when encountering an enemy, hardened criminal, or obnoxious acquaintance, we must react to more than what frightens or disgusts us. These people are human beings, the handiwork of God, persons for whom Christ died. Evil is not inherent in who we are as originally created, but a spoiling intruder that gained access because of our wrong use of the God-given freedom of choice.

2. Humans are now sinners.

The "image" of God was granted universally to humans. It is the ability to reflect the divine being, or at least embody aspects of the divine attributes. This image still remains in us, even if it is now more potential than presently real. What is so apparent is that God's intent for human life and divine-human relations has been twisted and misdirected by us, with tragic results. Sin is all too real. It is more than a matter of a mild deviance; it is caused by more than simple human ignorance and mistakes. It is a matter of deliberate decisions to turn our backs, make our own rules, and go our own way in open defiance of God's will.

It is an amazing act of God that grants us the ability to defy the divine will. Apparently, the freedom necessary to allow us to truly love our Maker (without being forced to do so—which would hardly be love) is precisely why we also have the freedom to defy the divine will. We are caught between opportunities, created for life and love, and yet able to choose death and hate. It is a beautiful design, and yet, by human choice, it has turned out to be a sordid story.

The autobiography of Leo Durocher, *Nice Guys Finish Last*, states a philosophy that reflects an attitude toward life akin to the biblical understanding of the root of sin itself. Durocher apparently believed in rules, but also the right to test the rules by seeing how far they can be bent. If a player is sliding into second base and the ball is thrown wildly by the catcher into center field, he sees nothing wrong with falling on the runner "accidentally" so that the runner can not get up and go to third in time. For Durocher, that is not cheating, but "heads-up baseball." Long before there was baseball, Eve saw the forbidden apple as tempting fruit that likely would taste delightful if she could get away with sampling it. She thought that disobedience was a good way to look out for her own best interests, to indulge whatever appetites she had. God called it self-will, sin. The apple was eaten and paradise spoiled.

There have been many inadequate views of sin and evil by prominent thinkers in recent generations. Bernard Shaw diagnosed the negative in human life as a by-product of poverty. Some psychologists dismiss it as merely a thwarted libido. Evolutionists classify it as an imperfection that has developed in the race and may go away. But realism and biblical thought continue to insist that there is a radical wrongness endemic in the very structure of our individual and corporate lives, a wrongness with moral dimensions, social consequences, and eternal implications. This radical wrongness is now found in all humans, although it is not part of who they were created to be—or yet can be.

There are two ways of defining sin in Christian theology. One includes all human failure to measure up to the perfect will of God. The language of the Westminster Shorter Catechism states, "sin is any want of, lack of conformity unto, or transgression of the law of God." This approach includes any conscious or unconscious, deliberate or accidental "missing of the mark" of God's perfect will for us. The other definition of sin limits what can properly be called sin to a defiant human will. The only sinful actions are the ones resulting from human choice to deliberately violate a known law of God for selfish reasons. The first is found typically in the Presbyterian tradition, and the second in the Wesleyan/Holiness tradition. Both definitions are true in an important sense; neither is fully true alone. We are caught between them.

Deliberately chosen evil can only be overcome by an inner change of the person through a process of repentance, forgiveness, and life renewal by God. Ending all missings of the mark of God's perfect will necessarily awaits the arrival of heaven itself, when even our humanness will be dissolved into glory. In the meantime, the transforming grace of God offers a redirection of the human will which, while still not perfect in performance, is graciously counted as righteousness in God's eyes. This possibility of a redirected will was what John Wesley meant by Christians attaining "perfect love" in this present world—a true "sanctification" that is not ever a perfection of performance, but a cleansed relationship with God that is viewed by God as restored righteousness.

The complexity of sin goes beyond how it is defined and resolved in relation to individual believers. Evil not consciously chosen by us, particularly when the evil resides in the impersonal workings of institutions, requires special means of solution. It calls for knowledge of cause and effect and for the calculated and constructive use of political power. Required are insight into the role of social environment in human life and wisdom and courage to be involved in the necessary process of large-scale change in public life. Sin is reality, but no simple reality. It is tragic, but treatable. It is personal and social. It is ugly, but still redeemable. We are really caught—but not without hope.

The biblical vision of humans as sinners presupposes that we are made in the divine image and have since deteriorated into a rebellious and lost condition. Strangely, recognizing ourselves as sinners is to assert again our essential dignity as children of God, a dignity made all the clearer when the darkness moves in to try to extinguish the light. Biblical teaching concerning sinfulness is not meant to belittle us and drive us into despair. The intent is to assist us to become so aware of the extent and nature of the true problem that redemption becomes a possibility— our prayerful and grateful choice.

To see humans only as reflections of the image of God is to miss the real world and become deluded by shallow optimisms. The twenty-first century is filled with illustrations of this danger. On the other hand, to see humans only as sinful is to lose sight of the deepest essence of our created nature and thus force a premature and unjustified cynicism. To see us as potential participants in God's plan of salvation is admirable and appropriate, but possible only when we are understood as a whole, when the paradox of our present being is fully embraced. Humans are fundamentally good (image of God), pervasively corrupted (original sin), and yet constantly the object of God's loving and seeking grace. Only in the light of divine grace can we understand the full meaning of our sin or ever hope to move back toward a place where its destructiveness can be swallowed up by forgiveness, love, and joy.

3. Humans are the recipients of a redemptive plan.

The supreme evidence of human worth to God is seen in that "while we were yet sinners Christ died for us" (Rom. 5:8). The Christian estimate of the problem and the possibility for us is seen in Christ's revelation of perfect humanity, and in his willingness to make the ultimate sacrifice for its restoration in each of us. God so loved that he gave. . . (Jn. 3:16). In the daily life of Jesus we are able to see sacrifice motivated by love. In him we can see goodness rising from trust and gratitude, instead of from the pressure of law, the hope of reward, or the fear of punishment. We know that what we see in Jesus is what we ourselves are meant to be. The good news that has come in Jesus is that what we were meant to be we yet can be!

Between License and Liberty

In Jesus Christ, believers are caught between freedom and slavery; we are truly liberated to a life of obedient service. The more we are emptied, the fuller we become!

There was a heated issue debated often as Paul traveled the ancient Mediterranean world and proclaimed his new faith in Jesus as God's Christ for us. Jews historically were committed to Torah, the Law of God. Paul was a highly trained Jew who, in his teaching about new life in Jesus, seemed to be violating the sacred Jewish tradition by suggesting a radical new freedom from the law. Does freedom from religious law, demanded his Jewish critics, not mean irresponsible and ungodly license?

We see in Jesus the living of a quality of life that we are encouraged to accept as a model for our own. It is characterized by the word *freedom*. But freedom in Jesus is not absolute—as it never is. Paradoxically, to understand the freedom to be found in Christ, we must find ourselves *caught between freedom and slavery*. Christian freedom is a freedom to be entered only as we choose to surrender our wills to the divine will. In effect, paradoxically, the more captive we become to the divine will the freer we know ourselves to be. Such captivated freedom may sound like nonsense to someone who thinks that freedom involves independence from all outside control. But, to the person of faith who recognizes the essential nature of humans as creations of God, it is clear that freedom is not finding independence as much as it is *choosing the proper dependence*.

St. Augustine, Martin Luther, and other famous Christians have been quoted often as saying things like, "The Christian life is basically loving God and doing as you please." Such statements are dangerous when taken out of their intended context. Still, they capture a very basic truth. As a Christian becomes committed to purity of heart and develops discipline in doing of God's will, what increasingly is experienced is freedom to do as one pleases— because, increasingly, one pleases to live in harmony with God. In this harmony arises true and intended identity as a creature of and co-creator with God. Only out of such yieldedness can there arise real human fulfillment. Since we were created in God's image, fallen though we now are, we become fully ourselves only as the curse of that fallenness is dissolved through renewed relationship with God. Such renewal leads us to the beautiful mystery of divine grace.

The most significant paradox of all is the *paradox of grace*. The Christian knows that every good thing comes from the hand of God. There are those verses in Romans 8 that speak of "predestination," even seeming to imply that there is a terrible selectiveness in God's love. Since God is God, all final choosing is his. Even so, would a loving God choose some people for salvation and doom others to destruction? Paul never intended these few words about predestination to be taken out of context and by themselves. That would make them argue for what he expressly resists elsewhere in his writings. Rather, the "election" words in Romans 8 are almost Christian poetry. They are seeking to celebrate a basic awareness among Christians. The humbled heart is keenly conscious that God has taken the initiative for our salvation. Hope of salvation roots only in the self-chosen sacrifice of a truly sovereign and also truly loving God. In fact, God's love predestines us all to salvation, unless we insist otherwise by our own choosing.

Praise is due unto God alone! And yet, in ascribing all to God, the Christian does not find it necessary to belittle human personhood or relinquish initiative and responsibility. As D. M. Baille says, "Never is human action more truly and fully personal, never does the agent feel more perfectly free, than in those moments of which he can say as a Christian that, whatever good was in them, it was not his but God's."[9] The amazing prayer of St. Augustine speaks of God being all in all: "Give what Thou commandest, and command what Thou wilt."[10] We are dealing with a God who commissions and enables—but without undercutting human integrity or responsibility in the process. It is the same as that paradoxical wisdom shared by Paul in Philippians 2:12: "Work out your own salvation because God is at work in you."

Note the delicate relationship between denying and affirming. Dietrich Bonhoeffer's classic observation picks up a theme often distorted by other well-meaning Christians. He observed that "when Christ calls a man, He bids him come and die.... In fact, every command of Jesus is a call to die."[11] What appears to be an opposing thesis is that persons can only love their neighbors when first they accept and love themselves. Did Jesus not say that we are to love our neighbors *as ourselves*? Here we have a polarity within which a believer discovers two of the basic truths of salvation. Deny thyself; love thyself.

Self-denial is a central element of Jesus' teaching. It is a basic condition for discipleship (Matt. 16:24; Mark 8:34; Luke 9:23). What is important to note, however, is that this denying does not mean that we necessarily are to deny ourselves *of something* (cake during Lent or a weekly night out). Nor does it mean that we are to assume that the human self is of no worth and therefore must be degraded and subdued so that a "spiritual" virtue can emerge. Rather, what Jesus had in mind was a call for wayward people to reject the foolish and idolatrous attempt of the self to be authentic and happy *by itself*, quite apart from God.

The church has always recognized the need for both affirmation and negation in the spiritual life of believers. The spiritual norm is "the balance between the divine and the human, the inner and the outer, the negative and the affirmative, the mystical and the practical, the monastic and the vocational."[12] As we die, we grow. Maintaining this balance is always a struggle. Life *as a whole* is to be caught up in the journey of faith.

It is interesting to contrast the two aspects of the life of Jesus seen in the words "he emptied himself" and "fullness" (Phil. 2:7 and Col. 1:19). Here is a strange converging of concepts. The fullness turns out to have dwelled in the One who previously had emptied himself. Gaining comes after losing. Christians, by God's grace, are called to reverse the tragic and selfish decision of Adam and Eve (of us). We are to act in faith on the fact that we humans find our true selves, our real freedom, our real happiness and fullness, only as we choose to empty ourselves of self-orientation and allow God to take the lead, set the bounds, and open the doors to new life and destiny. Those who empty themselves of themselves become full! We are caught in the paradoxical rhythm of emptying and filling, letting go and receiving back. Repentance leads to rebirth; obedience leads to freedom.

Most artists seek to create that which pleases the senses of others. Whether it is a painting, symphony, or well-designed building, the artist attempts to capture the attention and admiration of those who observe. It is the opposite with a magician. This art form consists mainly in hiding the actual practice of the art. Since the real skill is deception, the magician is only successful when managing to conceal what is really going on. The skill is in diverting attention so that there will be surprising, puzzling, and highly entertaining results. We look to the left and. . .surprise! Look at what we have on the right.

Similarly, the Christian directs attention away from self-preoccupation. However, in this case the purpose is not to deceive, but to give credit where credit is due. Christian people choose to bask in the grace of Jesus Christ, willingly engaging in genuine self-denial. But surprise! With such self-denial there emerges a self-affirmation of rare quality. If you do your praying with a pietistic flare on the front steps of the church, you will get your reward—they will see you, in fact, probably see straight through you for the hypocrite you are (Matt. 6:5). On the other hand, if your praying is done in a closet because your treasure is elsewhere, you will be rewarded openly. As you empty yourself for Christ, you become full.

Jesus said, "If any want to become my followers, let them deny themselves and take up their cross and follow me" (Mark 8:34). Then it happens. Suddenly we also hear, "You shall love your neighbor as yourself" (Mark 12:31). Releasing oneself into the superintendency of God apparently results in a most positive self-affirmation and the affirmation of others, a reverting to the earlier state when God looked at the creation, including humans, and, behold, it was very good (Gen. 1:31). Losing sight of oneself in a self-giving way results in the discovery and enhancement of one's own self.

The constant pursuit of happiness is not how happiness is usually found. Paradoxically, it is only when the seeds of the sinful self are hidden in the ground of God and allowed to die that the flower of the fulfilled and fruitful self can find birth. Only as God, by sheer grace, grants a sense of profound acceptance and security does the humbled child of God become free from self-preoccupation. Only then is the believer really able to relate in love to others. A person is not capable of loving others until there is a basis on which one can love and respect oneself. In fact, with the love and grace of God in mind, "one could say that the courage to be is the courage to accept oneself as accepted in spite of being unacceptable."[13] God so loved us that the divine love has transformed us, and now we can really love others in God's name.

Note the relationship between the paradox of grace and the place of human responsibility. What happens to our accountability if God is the one who commands and commissions, equips and enables? What if we are never required to be successful, only obedient, if all is of God and nothing is of us? Do we even need to engage in loving relationship and good works if salvation is through grace alone and not by virtue of any accumulated merit of our own? Do we need to work for what is a free gift?

Earlier we saw that humans fell into the bondage of sin and death because they sought freedom falsely and found the opposite of what was sought. Now, to regain proper standing before God and finally discover the only true freedom, we must willingly accept the restrictions and responsibilities of a unique bondage. There is an important sense in which only the losers in life will ever win. Only slaves will ever be free. Their freedom will be *in* and *because of* their slavery to Jesus Christ, not in their attempts to escape it. To yield is to be wonderfully released. The release is a divine gift. We cannot work to earn it; but, once received, we happily work because of it.

Paul says that a Christian is both the bondslave and the freeman of the Lord (1 Cor. 7:22). With the slave system of the Roman Empire in mind, Paul gives the general instruction that slaves who are converted to Christ should serve Christ where they are rather than seeking to escape from their masters, using Christ as the excuse to disrupt the social order. He instructs believing slaves to gain their freedom legitimately if that is possible. But, more importantly, they are to serve Christ with joy in whatever lot is theirs. Then he announces the paradox. When a slave becomes a Christian, he or she becomes the Lord's free person, having been delivered from the bondage of sin and death. When someone not a slave becomes a Christian, that person becomes Christ's slave, owing complete loyalty and service. In Christ, then, freedom and slavery are joined. Life in Christ becomes a liberated discipleship. It is a *joyous bondage* that lays heavy demands on each disciple, but without ever implying that salvation is granted on the basis of doing good works. Freedom is solely a matter of grace.

The paradox is that freedom is gained only through servitude. The believer freed in Christ is required by the very nature of this freedom to serve in complete obedience. The kingdom of Christ "is a kingdom not of oppressive control but of dreamed-of freedom, not of coercive dominance but of liberating love, not of top-down domination but of bottom-up service, not of a clenched iron fist but of open, wounded hands extended in a welcoming embrace of kindness, gentleness, forgiveness, and grace."[14] But this gentle Jesus is no puny pushover. To confess that "Jesus is Lord" is to make a strong political statement. This "powerless" Jewish rabbi of long ago is conqueror of all the Caesars who have ever reigned in this world. They are gone; he still reigns!

Believers in Jesus are really free—but hardly free to do anything. Writing to the Christians in Asia Minor, Peter distinguished between license and liberty, describing his readers as free precisely because they were servants of God (1 Peter 2:16). The Christian is the most free of persons, increasingly free even of the self. But the Christian is also a most dutiful servant, a profound debtor, subject to all for the sake of Christ. We Christians are free even from the law, except that freedom and law go hand in hand. We are free—free to obey! We all are slaves, having only the freedom to choose our masters. The Christian has chosen a master in whose service is found the freedom of abundant life.

The relationship of faith and works in Christian life illustrates this abundant life. In many biblical passages, the theme of "salvation through faith alone" is the only trumpet blast heard. Particularly is this so with Paul who tended to go almost to the extreme in one passage, only to balance the picture in some other passage (parallel passages must be held together!). In the book of James we hear little about faith and far more about works and their intimate relationship to authentic salvation. After running this maze of contrasting biblical passages, looking for a synthesis from a seeming thesis and antithesis, we must be patient until we see the composite biblical picture, in this case the paradox that *salvation is by faith alone,* but *saving faith is never alone.* It is accompanied by loving deeds that are the natural self-expressions of a saving faith in Jesus Christ.

By God's grace, people reborn in Jesus Christ are liberated from the curse of mechanical obligation to some distant, demanding power. By virtue of that very grace and liberation, such people are moved to obey whatever God's will might suggest. The Lord's Prayer starts with "Our." Obedience extends to the whole human family. "If anyone says, I love God, and hates his brother, he is a liar" (1 John 4:20). It is not enough to wear out our knees in constant prayer. We must rub shoulders, deal with the marketplace, demonstrate practical caring when and where such caring is most lacking. A few words from a special prayer composed for the Lambeth Conference of 1948 express the concern very well:

> Almighty God, give us grace to be not only hearers, but doers of thy holy word, not only to admire, but to obey thy doctrine, not only to profess, but to practice thy religion, not only to love, but to live thy gospel.

The Impossible Possibility

We humans are not merely to act differently; we are to be different. In this old world, we are to represent a new age that has dawned.

Many people have despaired of ever being a Christian because they think the standards of behavior are much too high to be attainable. As a matter of fact, these standards actually seem to be nothing short of moral perfection. As we read through Jesus' Sermon on the Mount (Matt. 5-7), we hear Jesus imposing a total demand on his followers. He forbids not merely the results of anger, but anger itself, not merely the act of adultery, but even adulterous thoughts. Such demands call into question more than a person's outward conduct; they place a spotlight on the very nature of a person's inner being. They insist, not simply that we *do* differently, but that we actually *be* different. They lay an ultimate claim on us, almost as if the fall of Adam and Eve had never affected us, as if our lives had risen above the corruptions of this present age. They do so because Jesus was proclaiming that *another age had dawned,* and because we believers now are expected to become living fruit of this new reality. We are caught between the truths of our fallenness and the high calling in Christ Jesus.

The Christian is intended to be conscious of two interlocking, overlapping realities. These may be expressed in the paradoxical statement, "I must die one day, but I will never cease to live!" Through faith in God's self-revealing and sacrificial work in Jesus Christ, the Christian knows that the dread of death itself died when Easter morning dawned. When the One who is the essence of life left the tomb behind, a way to eternal life was opened for all persons who will yield, love, and obey this amazing, life-giving God.

But there is more. With Easter morning there dawned the actual presence among us humans of that age that is yet to come. What *shall be* already *is,* at least in part. God's kingdom, the perfect divine rule, walked among us in the person of Jesus, lives with us now in the ministry of the Holy Spirit, and is to be seen emerging in the lives of faithful Christians. The Christian life is the *impossible possibility.* It is not possible by our own virtue or in our own strength. It is possible only as God lives the divine life in and through us. The witness in Galatians 2:20 is clear: "it is no longer I who live, but it is Christ who lives in me."

A Christian is a person who has been converted—not only *from,* but *to.* What is left behind are the idols of the past (1 Thess. 1:9) and the darkness of Satan (Acts 26:18). What is discovered are the elements of a bright new dawn. Basically, we turn "to the Lord" (Acts 9:35, 26:20), which is really a returning "to the Shepherd and Guardian of their [our] souls" (1 Peter 2:25). We show our backs to guilt and defeat and face squarely forgiveness and the source of victory, for now and forever. Such conversion centers in Jesus Christ. Note this clear statement:

> I am a Christian because I have confidence in Jesus Christ.... I trust Jesus. I think Jesus is right because I believe God was in Jesus in an unprecedented way. Through Jesus I have entered into a real, experiential relationship with God as Father, and I have received God's Spirit into my life.... As I seek to follow Jesus as my leader, guide, and teacher, I believe I am experiencing life in its fullest dimensions.[15]

With such conversion to Jesus Christ comes a double offer, the forgiveness of sins because of Christ and the gift of the Spirit of Christ (Acts 2:38, 3:19, 5:31).

Life in Christ is both a matter of release from the past and a lease on a new future. The problem is that some believers never get over the past, and some cannot get their minds off their new birth. Of course, the new birth is crucial and well worth celebrating. Without it we are not Christians at all. After we are reborn, however, the delight of that experience must lead into the larger concerns of growing into and living out this new life. To be born is only the beginning! To be born brings new freedom, freedom that should not be static and passive. Here are three key emphases related to Christian freedom.

1. A Christian is free—but not to follow his or her own will.

Freedom is mere chaos if it is made to mean that what we do is a matter of relative indifference. As a matter of fact, Christians are called *to live* in Christ; to those so alive, it is God's will that always makes the difference and shows the way. Christ is the redeemed person's new environment, the soil in which we grow, the air we now breathe. Christ's goals become our goals. Life comes to mean Christ to us (Phil. 1:21). We are free in Christ to think with him and love like him and work with him toward the completion of his tasks. By choice, we are no longer our own—*we are his.*

2. A Christian is free—but not to be silent.

We will never retain the saving grace of God by hoarding it, burying it for safekeeping, or seeking to protect it from contaminating contact with the poisons of the world. We retain the grace of God by risking it, acting on its promises, yielding to it daily, and announcing its good news as we have opportunity. To really believe is to actually be in Christ and really do through active witness to Christ. Doing is not optional. Put in terms of whimsical verse:

> God gave you so-called ends—
> One to think with and one to sit on.
> Success depends on the one you use—
> Heads you win and tails you lose![16]

Some Christians seek to serve Christ without ever bringing to the attention of others the issue of who Christ is and what role he is playing in their reasons for witness and service. However, we must not allow ourselves to live in troubled times and around dying souls without announcing the source of our own life and joy. If you are Christ's, you must say so! Elton Trueblood is so right in insisting, "there is no gospel without mission, and there is no mission without message."[17]

3. A Christian is saved—but not yet.

One of my New Testament professors had trouble with Christian testimonies that announce, "I am saved." The nature of our human situation will not permit any period-like punctuation mark related to such a statement since it suggests finality in this life. However, to say "I am saved" and follow it with a comma is the good news of a child of God who has experienced spiritual rebirth and is growing up into the full stature of Christ. We are disciples still in the making. Saying "I am saved" and following it with a period is often a subtle form of arrogance and the seed of spiritual stagnation.

It is obvious from the witness of Philippians 3:1-7 that, even in a seasoned Christian disciple like Paul, there was still a combination of rest and restlessness, serenity and striving, accomplished deliverance and continuing discontent. New birth was real; nurture and growth were yet needed. On the lips of every great Christian saint ever known by me were humble words of honest confession, such as "not that I have already attained," or "the more I know the more I realize how very little I really know," or "I believe, help my persistent unbelief."

We humans are granted salvation only by the gracious hand of God. As we approach this spiritual reality, our sense of timing is critical. Note the several tenses of salvation as presented in the New Testament. We *were* saved (Rom. 8:24). We *are being* saved (1 Cor. 15:2). We *shall be* saved (Rom. 5:9). Paul shares this whole time range in one verse: "Therefore, being justified by faith, we have peace with God through our Lord Jesus Christ; through whom also we have access by faith into the grace wherein we stand, and rejoice in hope of the glory of God" (Rom. 5:1). Paul is thinking of salvation: (1) as a looking backwards to the time when the believer received God's forgiveness in Christ and to those historical events that made it all possible; (2) as a rejoicing in the present realities of the "grace wherein we stand"; and (3) as a looking forward in faith to the time when we shall be like Christ, when every knee shall bow, and when sin and death will be no more. Our salvation *was* provided, *is being* sustained, and eventually *will be* fully realized. We were, we are, and we will be saved. All tenses are necessary, interact, and constitute the fullness of salvation. We are caught in the midst of all these tenses!

You Keep What You Give Away

Salvation is by faith alone, but saving faith is never alone. Christian life is a pure gift from God; it also requires all that we have to give.

The life of a Christian is one of high privilege and equally high responsibility. It is not so much that *we* now are alive as it is that *Christ* is now alive in us (Gal. 2:20). We have come to know by experience that, as we walk with Christ through this world, the "straight and narrow way" is as comprehensive as it is restrictive. It is as complex as it is uncompromising. Even in the midst of the unanswered questions and hard daily decisions, the Christ-life is simple and satisfying, while it remains full of majesty and mysteries.

The Christian way of living lends itself to misinterpretation by the average observer who does not share in Christ's life. Such is the case in part because this unique life has an additional dimension that turns upside down the usual values and expectations of the public. The basics of Christian living sound so paradoxical, so backwards from the normal run of popular thinking. We Christians pray prayers of genuine concern for our enemies. Most believers pray for the miracle of God's healing of physical ills and also turn to the best medical assistance available. The Christian community has always believed that what we keep we finally lose, and what we give away we still have. We are often overheard praying as though all depended on God. Then we cease our praying and go to work as though all depended on us. We sing with confidence that "little is much when God is in it." We also say with confidence that "you can't out-give God."

There is the old story of a man who struggled to reclaim a rocky and weed-covered piece of ground around his home. Finally, after months of hard work, there began to grow the loveliest of flowers and vegetables. One evening he was showing a friend around his now attractive and fruitful yard. His friend said, "It's wonderful what God can do with a piece of ground like this, isn't it?" "Yes," replied the owner, "but you should have seen it when God had it all to himself!" As German Christians say so well, this Christian life is both *Gabe und Aufgabe*, a gift and a task. It is all of grace, and yet, paradoxically, it requires all that we have to give.

To those who do not hear a divine drumbeat behind the surface noises of life, and who do not share the Christian's wonderful foretaste of the age yet to come, the attitudes and actions of Christians may seem strange and even foolish. Erasmus captured some of this in a famous satire:

> Lastly, no fools seem to act more foolishly than do the people whom zeal for Christian piety has got possession of; for they pour out their wealth, they overlook wrongs, allow themselves to be cheated, make no distinction between friends and enemies, shun pleasure, glut themselves with hunger, wakefulness, tears, toils, and reproaches; they disdain life and dearly prefer death; in short, they seem to have grown utterly numb to ordinary sensations, quite as if their souls lived elsewhere and not in their bodies. What is this forsooth, but to be mad?[18]

What is it? It is simply ordinary people who have discovered an extraordinary dimension of living. The deep-set guilt and dividedness in their lives had begun to fade in the face of their Creator who had come to live within. They knew themselves to be both the crisis and crown of creation. By the grace of God, "crown" was now in control. The crisis was being resolved by grace, so that one day soon, when the tragedy of all creation comes to a point of final judgment, those who have known the Creator personally as both judge and redeemer will be granted ultimate fulfillment in the divine presence. Rather than foolish, this is fabulous! Casual observations of others can bring judgments about them that are very wrong.

It has been said that "middle age" is that time of life when you do not have to have fun to enjoy yourself. This humorous observation illustrates a central characteristic of the Christian life. The Christian has entered into a dimension of life, a level of human existence in Christ guided by a unique perspective and posture. For the most part, daily circumstances have lost their power to jolt joy from its throne. Life runs deep and is fed by springs of living water that never cease to flow. Christians have seen light beyond the grip of death. We have discovered hope even in the midst of the pressures of life. There is a future, a goal to be reached, a crown to be worn. More than that, through the coming of Jesus Christ and our spiritual rebirth in him, we have been privileged to enter into the *presentness* of what is *yet to come*, the *now-ness* of the *shall be*!

There is so much talk among Christians about "eschatology" (end things). A common preoccupation is speculating about exactly how everything will finally work out. This intense curiosity, this presumably informed looking ahead is a big money-maker for numerous television prophets, book writers, and film makers. They are correct that the future is secure in God; but they are wrong in their level of supposed knowledge of the details of the future. They lose critical focus when attention is taken away from the central concern of Jesus—that we disciples be faithful *in the meantime*.[19] Our awareness of an assured future is intended by God to impact the quality of faithful discipleship lived out in the present. We know and we do not know about the ultimate tomorrow. In that paradox, we are to live the Christ-life now.

The real concern of the Book of Revelation "is not primarily for us to work from the present to the future, from the experience of Christ to the hope of His return, but from the certainty and nature of His end-time consummation to its meaning for the church in the present."[20] What do we know for sure about that final tomorrow? We know *whose* it is and we know *who* is with us now. They are one in the same! Past and future are secure in Jesus Christ, who is *alpha* and *omega*. We live between then and now. We are caught between assured hope and continuing questions and present responsibilities. In this caughtness, the call of Christ is for us to live the new life in him *now*. He will take care of the future.

Given the new life in Jesus Christ and the call to be on mission for him in this present world, the next chapter turns to the subject of the church. God's people are to be present examples of the Christ-life. They also are to be on mission, carrying the joy and spreading the good news.

Notes

1. David Elton Trueblood, *A Place To Stand* (N.Y.: Harper & Row, 1969), 47, 49.
2. Poem titled "The Road Not Taken" by Robert Frost.
3. Milton Berle, *Milton Berle: An Autobiography* (New York: Delacorte Press, 1974), 16.
4. Dietrich Bonhoeffer, *Letters and Papers from Prison* (New York: Macmillan, 1953), 221.
5. Reinhold Niebuhr, *The Children of Light and the Children of Darkness* (New York: Charles Scribner's Sons, 1944), xiii. Italics added for emphasis.
6. Samuel M. Powell, *A Theology of Christian Spirituality* (Nashville: Abingdon Press, 2005), 106.
7. Poem called "Purity" by Billy Collins, in *Sailing Alone Around the Room* (N.Y.: Random House, 2002), stanzas 1 and 2, page 40.
8. William Barclay, *Flesh and Spirit*, an examination of Galatians 5:19-23 (Nashville: Abingdon Press, 1962), 22.
9. D. M. Baille, *God Was In Christ* (New York: Charles Scribner's Sons, 1948), 114.

10. St. Augustine, *Confessions*, X:29.

11. Dietrich Bonhoeffer, *The Cost of Discipleship* (New York: Macmillan Company, 1948), 79.

12. Robert E. Webber, *Ancient-Future Faith* (Grand Rapids: Baker Books, 1999), 130.

13. Paul Tillich, *The Courage To Be* (New Haven: Yale University Press, 1952), 156.

14. Brian D. McLaren, *A Generous Orthodoxy* (Grand Rapids: Zondervan, 2004), 83.

15. McLaren, *A Generous Orthodoxy*, 69.

16. Theologian Rob Staples repeated this limerick to the internet Wesleyan Theological Discussion Group (December 2005), saying that a teacher had shared this with him this when he was in the eighth grade.

17. D. Elton Trueblood, *The Validity of the Christian Mission* (New York: Harper & Row, 1972), 98.

18. Desiderius Erasmus, *The Praise of Folly* (Princeton University, paperback edition, 1970), 118.

19. For an extensive study of Christian eschatology, see Barry L. Callen, *Faithful in the Meantime* (Nappanee, Ind.: Evangel Publishing House, 1997).

20. Frank Carver, "The Nature of Biblical Prophecy," in H. Ray Dunning, ed., *The Second Coming* (Kansas City: Beacon Hill Press of Kansas City, 1995), 25.

Church—Between Heaven and Earth

Christianity, beyond being a unique way of thinking, is a unique way of linking. The church is blessed with a measure of divinity, and also lives with much humanness.

Christians are caught between two unyielding facts when sharing their faith. They must be true to the faith's historic foundations and also sensitive to what it will take to communicate effectively that ancient faith to contemporary hearers. To fail in the first is to have the wrong message; to fail in the second is to have the message barely heard at all. This caughtness is seen in the opening verses of the First Epistle of John. The writer begins with "that which was from the beginning" (1:1), intending a faithful adherence to the young Christian tradition and its long Hebrew heritage of believing. The biblical writer also was adapting the Johannine tradition (e.g., the Gospel of John) to the altered needs of the believers he knew and was hoping to influence. He was being faithful to the past and to his present.

The church of every generation must do the same. The church of Jesus Christ is the body of people so caught between yesterday and today. Its roots reach back to Jesus himself and are nourished by all the saints of all past. Its commission is to cherish this past and embody its redeeming meanings in the setting of today. Its challenge is to do so with integrity and effectiveness. By referring to the church as the body of "resident aliens," current writers have meant that the church is to be a people very different from the world, thus aliens. They also are to be very much in and for the world, thus resident.[1]

Recently I visited a local congregation of Christian people that has been worshipping in the same location for decades. A large percentage of the church's present membership is made up of older people, many of whom carry memories of better times when the church was larger and the tone more "spiritual." The building is old and the community economically depressed. Over the objections of some members, the church's pews are new and padded, and the carpet is thick, red, and wall-to-wall. There is a history of deep concern for missions, *foreign* mostly, and of authoritarian pastors who have been culturally and doctrinally conservative. Its future is uncertain.

Any sensitive Christian person looking closely at any one of thousands of similar church situations would probably come to the same conclusion. The church is a *divine* institution, to be sure. Our faith, our stewardship, and at least some aspects of our lives together as Christians help to make that clear. Believers are not operating merely on the momentum of their own structures and programs. People have been changed through Jesus Christ and something quite unique has developed. It is the church. The church is blessed with a measure of divinity, and it also lives with much humanness. It is caught between heaven and earth.

A Divine-Human Reality

Because the church is human, it is subject to the limitations of people and time; because it is divine, God enables it to rise above such persistent limitations.

While the church obviously has divine roots, dimensions, and impact, it is just as obviously conditioned by many human factors. Sometimes it seems to be dominated by the human. Many petty things influence personal relationships. Particular decisions are made because of limited information, the insistence of a strong personality, or who happened to be present and voting that day. Organizational structure is usually determined by historical precedent and is only as relevant to the accomplishment of God's work as the people comprising it are committed to that end. The levels of understanding, maturity, and commitment vary widely among people who call themselves Christian.

What, then, is the church? The church is a gathering of people, ordinary people who have experienced divine grace. They are people with continuing limitations, people just down the street, but people who have been privileged to find new life in Christ and new fellowship with each other. The church has human organization, sometimes relevant and effective in implementing God's work and sometimes not. Always, the church is God's people seeking to be the divine "body" in this world. The members pray that God might reign in their hearts, speak through their words, act through their structures, in short, be in them and through them for their own sake and for the sake of all humankind.

After the bodily departure of Jesus from this world, there was a "colony of heaven" left behind to carry on his mission. This colony is the church, indwelled by Christ's Spirit who conveys gifts to the members to make possible their special life and task. Focus should be less on the humanness of church members and more on the power of God at work in and through them. On that first Easter, attention shifted from the earthly Jesus to the community of his disciples. Filled with the same Spirit, they shared significantly in the living, dying, and rising of Jesus. Accordingly, the church is the community of believers in Jesus who are on their way to Christ-likeness together through the ministry of Christ's Spirit. The church is the instrument of Christ, called to carry on his mission in the power of the Spirit.

Soon after the departure of Jesus from this earth, it was the church that confessed the divine "inspiration" of a particular set of writings. God's people had experienced the truth and power of God's Spirit through these writings, and thus had come to cherish them. There is a close relationship between the Bible and the church. In one sense, the Bible is the product of the community of faith that cradled its development. In another sense, it is the Bible that carried the message that brought the church into being. Paradoxically, the church that birthed the Bible is also the product of the Bible.

There are *three interlocking necessities* that must be characteristic of the Christian church if it is to be marked by the divine as well as the human. It must have: (1) a continuity with the past, especially with that decisive period recorded in the New Testament—be *apostolic*; (2) a willingness to profit from the whole of the Christian tradition, not just the isolated part where one happens to be associated—be *catholic*; and (3) the courage to critique, adapt, and act in the present as God may command—be *protestant*. Should the church be apostolic, catholic, or protestant? The right answer is "yes," caught among and blessed by them all.

When the church lacks any of these essential characteristics, there is a serious flaw in its makeup. Tradition and mobility may seem contradictory to those preoccupied with the past or floating aimlessly into the future, but in the life of the church they are complementary. A church with mobility but ignorant of its tradition has lost its roots and true identity. A church rich in tradition but lacking in mobility becomes a paralyzed prisoner of its own past. But the church that God calls and controls will be vitally in touch with the foundations of its heritage, adequately mobile for its present challenges, and constantly lured forward by a vision of the future that fulfills the past and gives direction to every new present.

There is a mystery about the Christian church. Theological vision and practical reality join to make necessary a paradoxical approach to the nature of the church. It involves the union of the human and the divine. Because the church is human, it exists at a given time and place with a given set of persons, all subject to the inevitable conditioning of those people and that moment in history. But, because of the church's divine element, it tends to move beyond and rise above the obvious human limitations. The church's humanness is conditioned by a new creation set in motion by God. The result is a body of frail but faithful people caught between heaven and earth, rooted in earth while en route to heaven.

The Church and the Churches

The church, despite its many diverse appearances in this world, remains mysteriously and somehow one.

Some real confusion has entered church history. Christians over the centuries have developed organizations that include many congregations and have referred to the organizations as "churches." This unfortunate terminology uses "church" in a way not anticipated by the New Testament. It takes attention and energy away from several crucial facts and mandates that are more basic than any contemporary human efforts to structure the life and work of God's people. Although the distraction is subtle and usually inadvertent, it nonetheless is damaging.

The New Testament employs the word *ecclesia* (church) often, usually with the words "God" or "Christ" related. The plural of "church" also occurs frequently, but is always a plural of distribution. It refers to the several local churches, such as the ones in Corinth, Philippi, Ephesus, etc. The word "church" never means denominations. Actually, Paul recoiled at the news that denominations had developed among the Christians in Corinth—a Paul-party, an Apollos-church, a Peter-denomination, even a Christ-party (1 Cor. 1:12; cf. 3:5). Human factors had surfaced to the point of causing division among Christians and distortion of their understanding of who they were to be as the church.

The church, while many with its diverse appearances, is to be *one*! It may be in many places and have many members, functions, styles, and organizational patterns, but it cannot be two or more bodies of Christ (cf. Rom. 12:4-8; 1 Cor. 12:12-30). Christians have been called into one body (Col. 3:15) and are intended to be members of that body (Eph. 5:30)—and therefore members one of another (Eph. 4:25).

Unfortunately, many Christians think of themselves primarily as members of a "church" (denomination), often dulling their awareness of the larger reality of the Body of Christ wherein their true membership lies.

To achieve the maximum level of visible Christian unity this side of heaven, individual Christian traditions should consider downplaying

> ...all narrow identifications related either to a church leader (e.g., Mennonite), church government (e.g., Presbyterian), church headquarters (e.g., Church of God–Anderson), a doctrinal distinctive (e.g., Baptist), a phenomenon (e.g., Quaker), an idealistic state (e.g., Reformed), a nation (e.g., the Church of England), or a function (e.g., Salvation Army), and identify themselves as closely as possible with the church of the New Testament.[2]

This is not to say that various traditions do not carry emphases needed by the whole church. It is only to say that such emphases should be presented as gifts to the whole, not function as walls dividing the whole.

One current Christian university seeks such a proper balance between denominational roots and its all-church vision, advertising itself as "historically orthodox, clearly evangelical, genuinely ecumenical, and distinctively Wesleyan."[3] In this range of designations is an appreciative sense of the entire Christian tradition, a desire to be "catholic" (ecumenical), all in the context of recognition of a particular Christian tradition, the Wesleyan, that is highlighted for the sake of the whole Christian heritage. A Christian theologian puts it well:

> The day for narrowly conceived, denominationally oriented systematic theologies is over. While my roots are deep in the Church of God (Anderson), they are not therein root bound; they extend into the rich heritage of the whole church. It used to be that, when I appreciated something about another tradition of the Christian faith, I wished it were mine as well. No longer is that the case. I now embrace it *as mine*.... The ancient and ever-widening circle of Christian disciples is invigorating, enriching, instructive, and challenging for all members of it who affirm not only a section of the circle but the whole of it.[4]

Differing beliefs, styles of worship, and cultural backgrounds cause Christians to cluster in various ways and function separately from each other. To an extent, this is inevitable and possibly even useful. But, to the extent that certain situations are sanctified by orienting the focus of our Christian lives around incidental circumstances, to that extent we have done violence to truth and harm to God's work. As Christians, our primary identity is *in Christ* and thereby *among his people*—all of his people! The church is to be a community extension of Jesus, a people modeling his grace and victory and sharing his good news. The power of the New Testament church rooted less in what it *did* and more in what it *was*, "a body which, through God's Spirit, united former enemies around the living truth, Jesus Christ."[5] The church was and still should be *one body* of transformed believers on mission together in the world.

We cannot avoid the basic paradox of church membership. By virtue of our birthright as converted children of God, we are members of the whole church. By virtue of personal, family, geographic, and historical circumstances, we find our place to function in the life of the church by becoming associated with a particular historical expression of its life. We belong, at one time, to the whole and to part of the whole. The whole, without concrete and localized expressions of itself, is little more than a dream. But any concrete and local expression of the whole that is not defined by and oriented to the whole is an alien strain hurtful to the whole. We are caught between the whole and part of the whole.

Am I a Baptist or Methodist, a Roman Catholic or Presbyterian? Whatever the answer, the more important question is, Am I a Christian in loving fellowship with my brothers and sisters everywhere? Church membership should be in the one and only body of believers, the body of Christ. The "secondary membership" in a subdivision of the church's life should function on behalf of the church itself. If some voluntary association of Christians builds artificial and unnecessary walls between Christians, that association ceases to be a legitimate part of the whole and becomes a thing of its own, an obstacle to the whole. All formalized associations of Christians experience human limitations. Let all be self-critical and open to the wisdom of other brothers and sisters in the faith.

Since the church stands between heaven and earth, between the present evil age and the age to come (which is already coming in the church and its mission), it is critical to understand the in-betweenness of the church's life. With dual citizenship come dual responsibilities and a tension that always risks a tipping of the balance. The supernatural can become so dominant a preoccupation that the church loses touch with and even interest in the things of this world. All is thought to be of God in so immediate a way that the lessons of history, the laws of sociology, even the knowledge of modern medicine are set aside as irrelevant, human, earthly, somehow the opposites of faith. Practical ministry and timely mission suffer because of impatient hopes for heaven that short-circuit the here and now.

Too often, on the other hand, the church becomes captivated by itself and the tasks it has to accomplish. When this happens, the standards that are to measure success or failure become mostly the fruit of human dreaming. The means for achieving success become mostly the products of human scheming. God is relegated to the murky realm of distant memory and traditional religious vocabulary. While such self-oriented and socially-oriented persons remain within the church structure and continue to call on God's name in reference to their own efforts, they do so with decreasing passion and purpose.

Reinhold Niebuhr once reviewed the church's chronic ineffectiveness in influencing wayward political situations. He concluded that the tendency of the church is "to destroy the dialectic of prophetic religion, either by sacrificing time and history to eternity or by giving ultimate significance to the relativities of history. Christian orthodoxy chose the first alternative, and Christian liberalism the second."[6] There is a rhythm essential to the adequate existence of the church, a careful alternation of point and counterpoint, the natural and supernatural, the past and present, the substance and symbol, the local and universal. To emphasize any at the expense of the others is to break the rhythm and silence the divine music.

Jesus once announced, "You are Peter, and on this rock I will build my church, and the powers of death shall not prevail against it" (Matt. 16:18). He intended that his church should live at all times by doing what Peter did. Peter had seen God behind the figure of the carpenter's son from Nazareth and had openly confessed his faith in Christ as the Son of God, the foundation of a new fellowship of believers, the church. God's church must see with Peter beyond the usual human considerations to the foundational truth of the Christ and his on-going ministry in the world. Christ's faithful followers have genuine existence only as they relive that moment at Caesarea Philippi when Jesus was recognized and proclaimed to be the Lord.

Believers need to be aware and appreciative of the paradox of the two essential dimensions of church life, the *dynamic* (charismatic) and *stabilizing* (institutional forms and linkage with the church's historic traditions). These two dimensions can conflict, but ought to compliment each other. Stabilizing form is necessary in church life, although it is to be only a passing vehicle for the life and work of the Spirit of God. God gives spiritual gifts and brings new life, insight, and passion—the dynamic. Church members seek ways to remember the faith correctly and discipline community life for the sake of Christ's mission in the world—the stabilizing.

Paul reminded the Corinthian Christians that by typical human standards they had been nobodies (1 Cor. 1:26-29). Nonetheless, now they were "the body of Christ" (1 Cor. 12:27), the company of the committed who, by the power of God, were to continue the ministry of Christ in the world. Even as Jesus was a bridge person, participating in human existence and yet not limited to it, his disciples would be between heaven and earth, rooted in one, reborn in the other, abiding in one, agents of the other. The church is a community of hope, a present reality created by the impact of the future made known in the history of Jesus. It lives between the times and between the worlds.

Hate and Love "The World"

We simultaneously are to love the world and shun "worldliness."
We are to give to "Caesar" what is his—if we can figure out
what is his and what is God's alone.

Once the true identity of the church is clear, the next pressing question before the church becomes "Where?" Where shall the witness be made? Not "Whether?"—because there is no question that we must. Not "When?"—because we always must. Not even "How?"—because that will come to us in the process of our honest attempts to witness. The prior question is "Where?" Originally, the answer came from Jesus as follows: "You shall be my witnesses in Jerusalem and in all Judea and Samaria and to the end of the earth" (Acts 1:8); "Go therefore and make disciples of all nations" (Matt. 28:19).

The earliest Christian disciples supposed that they would stay in Jerusalem and in some constructive way associate themselves with the worship routines at the Jewish temple (Acts 5:42). Their original notion of mission was shaped by the assumption that the peoples of the world would come to Jerusalem and there be blessed by Christ through his people. But they finally realized the folly of this expectation. In fact, the fall of Jerusalem to the Romans in 70 A.D. clarified beyond all question that the fulfillment of their evangelistic commission must come in some very different way. The alternative way came to be a philosophy of diffusion rather than ingathering. All lands had to be seen as potentially the "holy land." There can be no settled and sacred Mecca for Christians, only new frontiers that cry out for the word of the gospel. There can be no one cultural pattern or racial stock. There is one gospel and one glorious church.

There also is our world. This place—"the world"—is a dilemma for Christians. We are taught to shun it when it comes at us as "worldliness."

We also are commanded to love it and seek its transformation since "God so loved the world" (Jn. 3:16). We are sometimes paralyzed by this paradox. Poet Billy Collins was once resting in the bedroom of an old farmhouse he had just purchased, thinking of those who had lived there before him. The house had been built during the Civil War by a man "with the strength of a dairyman and with the tenderness of a dairyman, or with both, alternating back and forth." With that family long dead, Collins pondered his own circumstances, "feeling better and worse by turns." Such paradoxical feelings often come to the Christian as attempts are made to apply the faith's implications to given social settings.

Christians have seen receiving the grace of God as the appropriate means of resolving the inner problem of selfish attachment to "the world." Recently, however, many of us have become aware of a coordinate truth about transformation. Mission to the public arena should be the necessary consequence of private renewal. People hold the nuclear scales of the planet's life or death in their unsteady hands. God has made us responsible for our share in human history.

Past centuries saw the typical self-understanding of persons focused on themselves as *subjects*. They belonged and obeyed. They tended to visualize themselves as passive responders to the forces of life. People were obedient citizens of the ruling powers. Sometimes these dictating forces were identified with the uncontrollable furies and bountiful harvests of nature. At other times it was the political powers in control or the prevailing religious and cultural traditions. But such relative passiveness is ceasing to be the way of human self-understanding.

People today tend to see themselves more as independent initiators and activists. New technical capacities have bolstered our ability to stand up to life and answer back. If rain is needed, make it. If a disease plagues people, do research and stop it. If the planet is severely overcrowded, develop ways to control births and even transport us to other worlds. If a society's institutions seem inadequate to meet the needs, the institutions should be changed. If the lifestyle of parents seems unsatisfactory, decide to "do your own thing." For good or ill, we are beginning to claim a larger share of responsibility for our own history. There may be some arrogance and unrealism in this, but we are encouraged by our many scientific and technological successes so far.

God is not separate from this determination and potential. History is the arena of God's action. The exodus from Egypt was not understood by the Hebrews as merely a successful labor revolt that gave them freedom to mold their own future. No! It was God at work on the historical scene, enabling their future according to the divine promise. To believe in the living God is necessarily to believe that God is at work in the world where people live and love, suffer and die. God is present where bodies are mangled by the machines of war and spirits are crushed by chronic poverty, where people hunger for bread, justice, and love, where they dig ditches in the dust and still reach for the sky in faith.

Despite such belief, Christians have found it easy to almost disregard the significance of human history. The tendency is to ignore the larger movements of humankind, preferring a private celebration of the love of Christ, dismissing on-going history as a mere backdrop for personal experiences of salvation. Purity tries to be protected by social isolation. A preoccupation with the end of the age and beyond sometimes deadens interest in engaging the present. Too many believers become *paralyzed by paradise*. Nevertheless, Christians in our world know that God is far from dead, and disciples of Jesus remain commissioned to relate themselves responsibly to the present fulfillment of divine goals.

Christianity lives in the paradox of *yesterday-today-tomorrow*. Since the road to the Christian future necessarily runs through the Christian past, Robert Webber titled his crucial book *Ancient-Future Faith*.[7] We are caught between yesterday's necessary *roots* and today's necessary *fruits*. Christians are people journeying together as the church with foundational memories and persistent hope. We are pilgrims whose final home is beyond this present world, but who have a mission in this world that drives us deep into its very life.

New Testament religion is very personal, but it is hardly private. It involves a church and a world. In John Wesley's blunt words: "Holy solitaries" is a phrase "no more consistent with the gospel than 'holy adulterers.' The gospel of Christ knows no religion but social; no holiness but social holiness. Faith working by love is the length and breadth and depth and height of Christian perfection."[8] There is no either-or option. The people of Jesus must have the vision and courage to live in some *both-and* realms. Although believers find peace with God one at a time, they must engage this world together as the church. It is *my* conversion; but *we* are the church.

Jesus is Lord! But Lord of what? I have struggled with the contention that the church somehow misapplies the lordship of Christ when using it as a stimulus for involvement in economic and political problems. Does Christ forbid the church to enter into the sphere of Caesar? Jesus seems to suggest separate jurisdictions of state and church. He declares that his kingdom is not of this world, that he is not a divider of wealth, and that the church should use only spiritual weapons in the fight against evil. Trying to achieve justice in the public sphere necessitates the strategic use of political power and involves difficult decisions with unclear "moral" implications. However, the alternative to meaningful engagement with crucial public issues is unthinkable. It is always time for *both-and*. The "whole counsel of God" is not recognized until we have affirmed the lordship of Christ over the larger worlds of learning, culture, and government.

The Christian community is obliged to press the divine claim upon the nations of the earth, including all the power structures devised to order public life. Jesus Christ still forgives sinners one by one and allots them individually a place in his kingdom; but this marvelous process of rebirth is the beginning of the story and *not the end*. The gospel that we celebrate is not an "individual gospel" any more than it is a "social gospel." It is a gospel that admits to no limits. It is a message of life for the total person, including every aspect of the world in which people live.

The Book of Revelation concludes the library of biblical materials by combining carefully the apocalyptic and prophetic traditions found sporadically throughout biblical materials. What is joined is a sober realism about the roots of power, the fruits of idolatry, and a stern call for Christians to be keenly aware and ethically responsible. Human history is indeed the arena of evil, the place of persecution; it also is the arena in which God has worked out human salvation and God's people are called to live redemptive lives. We are caught between what appear to be contrasting biblical views of human governments—they are deserving of our obedience (Rom. 13) and revolting in God's eyes (Rev. 13).

The dual mission of personal evangelism and social transformation raises urgent questions of motive and method. The church must not seek converts merely to enlarge and maintain its own institutions. It must not play statistical games with human souls. Nor must it relate to society's problems with an eye to gaining political control for itself so that it can impose its will on all people. It must not become fond of the use of power or totally shun its use. The church must never be deluded into thinking that morals can be legislated, nor must it allow itself to forget that enlightened legislation can be an instrument by which a society can educate and discipline itself for good or evil. The church must walk a fine line that necessitates delicate distinctions.

A major thread that runs through the many writings of Reinhold Niebuhr is his continuing struggle with the relationship between the *ideal* and the *real*. He recognizes the problem of the relationship between desired communities and the communities in which people actually live. There is continuing tension between Christian ideals for society and political cynicism that comes from involvement in what society actually is. As a Christian, Niebuhr's conclusion is neither to give up the ideals nor yield to the paralysis of cynicism. We must discover constructive ways of dealing effectively with the realities out of the vision of Christian ideals. For the Christian, the distance between what appears possible at any given time and the perfect divine will for that time is covered by grace. This grace-covered gap is an in-between situation, the difficult place where we must live courageously for Christ.

For the church living in this gap, there is another classic point of tension. What is the appropriate relationship between the church and the civil government or state? As Senator Mark Hatfield once said in reference to the United States, "We have taken the Constitutional doctrine of separation of church and state and converted it into a practice of separating the world of faith from the world of politics. The result is clear: our political system is threatened by a vacuum of moral values and the evangelical church is threatened by a vacuum of social relevance."[9] This kind of separation is not acceptable.

According to 1 Peter 2:18, we are to "fear God, honor the king, be subject to your masters, suffer for goodness' sake and God will bless you." But the larger context of the Bible and human experience tempers the apparent rigidity of this verse. Jochebed disobeyed civil authorities by preserving her son, Moses; Rahab betrayed her own government by assisting the spies from Canaan; Daniel disobeyed the king's decrees; Jeremiah preached boldly against disastrous government policies. All of them were blessed by God for their varying degrees of civil disobedience. Peter did write: "Be subject for the Lord's sake to every human institution." (1 Pet. 2:13). But, after one of his arrests by authorities for his own civil disobedience, he also said, "We must obey God rather than men" (Acts 5:29). Martin Luther rebelled and thereby helped initiate the Protestant Reformation; many German Christians later failed to rebel against their Nazi master and thereby contributed to the slaughter of millions of people.

The circumstance is paradoxical. Followers of Jesus Christ should not avoid the considerable risks of world penetration. Before the penetration, however, they must be shaped by Jesus Christ if they are to make a difference for the Lord instead of being absorbed by a resisting culture. Jesus is our model. He retreated in private prayer, dealing first with his own relation to the Father before merging back into the crowds. Then he knew who he was and what he was to do. Later transfigured on an isolated mountaintop, Jesus sent his disciples down into the valleys of human need (they preferred to stay in the spiritual euphoria, of course).

Purity and Penetration

We face the Elijah-Elisha paradox. God's people are to be defensive and offensive at the same time, maintaining the purity of the faith against the world's idols and addressing that same world wisely and persuasively.

A most difficult New Testament paradox involves the prepositions *in* and *of.* The Christian community is, at the same time, *in* this world as a witnessing presence and *of* another world in terms of the source, direction, and power of its own life. The resulting tension centers in trying to define the appropriate border between church and non-church. Christian faith stands in a twofold relation to the present world. It calls believers (1) to transcend the world's perverted values and ways of life and also (2) to participate constructively and redemptively in the same world.

We recall that Jesus viewed the functions of faithful disciples in terms of salt and leaven, caring more for penetration into the bastions of evil than for protection of the sacred places of the religiously devout. He saw the role of God's people less as a privileged group rescued from the world and more as a commissioned group bearing a special responsibility toward all humanity. This commissioned group is the church that is to have six key characteristics:

> First, Jesus is the source, center, and Lord of the church. Second, the church is holy. Third, it is a community, not a collection of lone rangers. Fourth, precisely because it submits to Jesus' kingdom norms, the church is a counter-cultural community living a lifestyle that fundamentally challenges worldly values and practices. Fifth, mutual accountability and responsibility are essential in this astonishing new social order. Sixth, only in the power of the Spirit is it possible for this new community to be the new righteous, counter-cultural social order that its Lord requires.[10]

As the centuries of church history have unfolded, Christians increasingly have come to appreciate more the significance of Christ's words to the woman at the well of Samaria: "The hour is coming when neither on this mountain nor in Jerusalem will you worship the Father" (Jn. 4:21).

There has been the tension between the tendencies toward penetration of the world in the name of Christ and retreat from the world to some safe place of local tradition and religious purity. There has been the temptation to view this world as a lost cause—so we chose to wait passively for the ultimate elimination of this world by Christ's return. This sterile kind of faith, however, ignores much of biblical revelation and undercuts much of the church's mission.

Purity and penetration form a classic pair of concerns that seem contradictory on the surface. It often is assumed that being involved with non-religious people and issues inevitably prostitutes one's own religious purity. Jewish religious leaders thought it a scandal when Jesus voluntarily spent time in sordid surroundings with prostitutes and tax collectors. It is crucial to see that purity and penetration are parallel concerns that comprise a crucial paradox. The Elijah-Elisha paradox is helpful.

The mission of Elijah was to maintain the purity of the religion of God's people by fighting all religious adulteration and destroying the encircling idolatry. By contrast, the mission of Elisha, his successor, was to be a prophet of power in which God was affirmed as active and sovereign in political life, reigning over kings and directing world affairs. The people of God are to be both pure (Elijah) and active on all fronts as agents of their God (Elisha). The mandate is not one or the other, but to be caught between them, affirming and living out both.

The first-century church, fired by Christ's commission and Paul's evangelical zeal, seemed to swing toward a preoccupation with world penetration. By contrast, the second-century church had a heightened sense of need for separateness that would protect its fragile life from the world's contamination. Surprisingly, it was not long before the new faith community was accepted as "official" in the Roman Empire. Becoming the establishment religion was a big danger to its continuing integrity. Both tendencies, plunging into the world with a wonderful message and keeping distance from the world for the sake of the integrity of the message, are valid Christian impulses. Swinging too far either way tends to destroy the higher truth that can be realized only in the maintenance of the tension. The tension is this. The church is under divine orders to come out of the world to strengthen its unique identity. The purpose for coming out is going in. The church is sent back into the world better equipped for mission effectiveness.

The work of the church should proceed by a delicate and dynamic uniting of individual piety and group action, a journey inward to the foundations of spiritual life and a journey outward to the concrete policies and procedures that introduce redemptive changes into the prevailing patterns of the world. In the dramatic life of Dietrich Bonhoeffer we see courageous action directed at the verbal poison and social madness that gripped the German people in the 1930s and 1940s. We also read this in a letter to his brother in 1935: "The restoration of the church must surely come from a new kind of monasticism, which will have only one thing in common with the old, a life lived without compromise according to the Sermon on the Mount in the following of Jesus."[11] Here was a Christian monasticism on mission in the world, monks without walls!

To be divine agents is difficult and invites misunderstanding and even persecution. A letter in *Newsweek* magazine pictured an awkward irony in two articles that it had printed earlier: "I am an American Baptist minister and the irony is one that all of us pastors face. Article one is about Pope Pius XII, who is being accused of 'playing politics' because he was silent in the face of injustice. Article two was about the 'social activism' of the ministers in the 1960s who are being criticized for 'playing politics' because they spoke out against injustice. Is it any wonder that so many ministers are bald?"[12] The wise message of John Wesley was one of personal salvation that necessarily leads to heightened social conscience. Conversion to Christ is two-sided. The *full* gospel includes religious zeal and social enthusiasm. Salvation is both intensely personal and passionately social.

Benjamin E. Mays was an outstanding African-American Christian who rose from bitter memories of slavery in South Carolina to being a mentor of Martin Luther King, Jr., and a valued advisor to American presidents. He raised difficult questions that the church must not ignore. Mays had struggled for many years to know how to live in a racially segregated society without accepting as normal and inevitable that which was "ugly, mean, stupid, and cruel." Then comes his admission: "Segregation in the House of God has been a great strain on my religion."[13] He was caught between the ideals of his faith and the realities of his world. He knew a church that concentrated on self-culture in spiritual matters and settled for indifference in other matters. Those Christians apparently longed for purity. They left out penetration. Their protected purity had lost its Christian character because it was detached from a vital piece of its own essence, responsible mission in the social arena. According to Psalm 85:10, "Steadfast love and faithfulness will meet; righteousness and peace will kiss each other." Only when spiritual purity and world penetration kiss is the faith fully itself and really relevant.

The basic question comes down to defining the task of the church. The answer turns out to be plural rather than singular. The church is to be *purist* and *penetrationist*, Elijah and Elisha. In his opening remarks as chair of the World Congress on Evangelism (Berlin, 1966), Carl F. H. Henry announced to participating Christian delegates from over one hundred countries that "the God of the Bible is the God of *justice* and *justification*. The Christian evangelist has a message doubly relevant to the modern scene; he knows that justice is due to all because a just God created mankind in his holy image, and he knows that all men need justification because the Holy Creator sees us as rebellious sinners."[14] Jesus never prayed that his disciples should be removed from the world. His concern was that the evil of the world should be removed from their hearts so that, as they were in the world, they would be able to present a genuine alternative to its misery and lostness.

The Christian community may be thought of as resident aliens in a foreign culture. Philippians 3:20 says that "our citizenship is in heaven." Being strangers in a strange land was something that Jewish Christians of the first century understood well. They remembered the Exile experience in Babylon and similar struggles under later Greek and Roman occupations. Today, for Christians in the Western world, the old "Christendom" is a dying reality. No longer will secularized societies privilege in its laws and schools the Jewish-Christian faith tradition. We are being moved back to the earlier situation where believers must be responsible for knowing their own religious traditions, educating their own young in the faith, and learning to swim against and serve within alien social tides.

Being a small beachhead on a large battleground implies a defensive posture, the need to survive and perpetuate a distinctive identity on foreign soil. For Christians, it also implies an offensive stance, the call to represent the first fruits of a new creation on mission in the world. Even though the church now lives in a religious buyer's market where the "customer" is king, it must avoid being a consumer-oriented organization that caters to the "fulfillment needs" of individuals. It must realize its "radical" nature as a counter-cultural body shaped and motivated by the story of God with us in Jesus Christ. It must reclaim the adventure of actually *being* the church, the gathering of changed people who live by grace as an alternative community. Such living inevitably signals to the world Christ's new life, a life that the world needs desperately, but cannot duplicate on its own.

To live and witness successfully as resident aliens requires sacrifice and discipline. According to Ephesians 6:10-20, Christian discipleship is costly. The central challenge is the formation of a visible people who know and accept the significant cost involved. The call is to be a church "asserting clearly that God, not nations, rules the world, that the boundaries of God's kingdom transcend those of Caesar, and that the main political task of the church is the formation of people who see clearly the cost of discipleship and are willing to pay the price."[15]

An essential Christian paradox joins personal transformation and a key role for the community of believers. Protestantism has leaned on a distinction that has been less than helpful—the *visible* and *invisible* church. The original concern was to distinguish between the flawed institutional forms of the church and the fellowship of all the truly converted, now alive and dead. The unintended result has been an excessive elevating of the invisible and a devaluing of the visible. If the visible church comes to appear optional, not tied clearly and necessarily to the whole salvation process and mission mandate, then "participation in it can quickly become, at best, motivated more by pragmatic considerations than by a sense of necessity, and at worst, merely a matter of personal preference."[16]

The paradox is that the church that *we see* is obviously both human and divine. Its boundaries are "invisible" because of its universality, but the church is nonetheless to be very visible. To be seen in the church is a refection of the person and work of God in Jesus Christ. The world will come to believe mostly by contact with what it sees as the actual, the visible truth of a truly Christian community existing in this world (Jn. 13:35). It is not enough for the visible church of today, with all of its organizational division and theological dissension, to be justified by reference to an ideal but invisible church reality. The world looks at the high claims of the Christian gospel and tends to judge the church on the results *here and now*. We must be, and be together, what we claim.

The Presentness of the Future

Disciples of Jesus live here in light of the hereafter. There must be no disconnect between now and then. We are to be faithful in the meantime.

The basic premise of an earlier book of mine[17] was that the kingdom of God both has arrived in Jesus and is not yet fully here. It is *near* and yet not altogether *here*. Christians have hope and are to live from that hope. Christian "eschatology" (doctrine of final things) is more than hoping for what is still to come. It is the call to be faithful *in the meantime* in light of what is believed to be coming. Such new life comes from the power of the present foretaste of that which will come. Any abandonment of the present time is an abortion of Christian mission in this world. We do not have all the answers about what lies ahead, and we do not need to know. We must stop speculating about future details and start serving now, living the Christ-life in the power of Christ's Spirit—who is already here.

The Bible calls for acting courageously in the present, and doing so with the resources of the future. Unfortunately, the discouraged of earth, and even the frightened disciples of Jesus, often retreat to the sidelines of public life, trying to avoid the realities and risks of the present. I am disturbed by the following poetic lines. It is said that clocks in saloons typically are set fifteen minutes ahead of the clocks in the outside world. According to saloon patrons:

> This makes us a rather advanced group,
> doing our drinking in the unknown future,
> immune from the cares of the present,
> safely harbored a quarter of an hour
> beyond the woes of the contemporary scene.[18]

How sad—and how wrong!

There is a tension as a Christian grows up into the stature of Christ and participates in the church's mission to spread the good news. One is caught between heaven and earth. The whole life of the believer is lived under the constant tension between the *now* and the *hereafter*, the part and the whole, momentary defeat and eventual triumph. Micah and Isaiah, ancient prophets living by faith in their troubled times, exhibited "an apparently inconsistent juxtaposition of uncompromising doom and unequivocal assurance."[19] Times are terrible—and redemption is sure!

For Christians, the clearest focusing of the paradox is seen in the life of Jesus. He taught that the kingdom of God was being realized in his time, particularly in conjunction with his own ministry. He also taught that this kingdom strained toward a final consummation beyond human history. We can only understand the mission of Jesus when we keep in view these two poles between which lies everything he said and did. The one pole is the conviction that the kingdom of God is future and not captive to the evils of this world. The other pole is the consciousness that this kingdom is already in the process of coming to realization in the very midst of this world.

The reign of God is here! The kingdom is not yet. Here is the paradox of present and future. The church is not the kingdom, but it should be deeply bound up with it. The church is made up of people seeking to be increasingly defined by the kingdom. It is the "eschatological community" already committed to living and proclaiming God's full and soon-to-be final rule. The church is a paradoxical body, human and divine, not an institution of earth and yet inevitably assuming institutional forms. The point is "to affirm the biblical richness, diversity, and mystery of the true body of Christ and to seek practical models that are both faithful to Scripture and highly relevant to the church's being today in its concrete socio-cultural context."[20]

How should the church, an emissary from elsewhere, conduct itself as it lives between heaven and earth, between here and hereafter? With some degree of indifference as people did at Laodicea (Rev. 3:14-22)? Nervously as was done at Thessalonica (2 Thess. 2:1-2)? Curiously as did many who kept pestering Jesus for signs? Or, with Paul, will the church be able to join "looking for the blessed hope and appearing" with the necessity of "living soberly and righteously in this present world?" Too often the church seems near death from an overdose of expectancy. We are blessed by hope—and called to live courageously in its light.

According to Jesus, the church should live in a surprising and even scandalous way. He had begun implementing awareness of a new kingdom, God's kingdom, by exposing the evil inherent in all alternative kingdoms. Most of the demons he faced and exposed were organized systems of power and violence—government (the Roman Empire), political movements (Zealots and Herodians), religious parties (Pharisees and Sadducees) and hierarchies (the high priests), and excessively demanding family systems ("let the dead bury their own dead," Matt. 8:22). Jesus' counter message was: "Just as sick, destructive spirits can take possession of groups, this new Spirit [the Holy Spirit] is entering people and forming them into a healthy, creative, and new kind of community or society—the kingdom of God."[21] This kingdom, emerging in Jesus, was not a religious tranquilizer that gets comfortable with evil or at least learns to endure it passively. It was a fire of love that confronts the wrong and models a better way.

The message of Jesus was a scandalous one, exposing the weakness of the supposedly powerful and the power of the apparently weak. Exposing evil, of course, brings the wrath of evil, leading to a crucifixion, the apparent defeat of Jesus' counter way of love and forgiveness. But, following the amazing resurrection of the dead Jesus, we now are left with a demanding paradox. The only way the kingdom of God can be its true self and express its distinctive strength "is through a scandalous, non-coercive kind of weakness; the only way it can be powerful is through astonishing vulnerability; the only way it can live is by dying; the only way it can succeed is by failing."[22]

Honoring this paradox at the heart of Christian faith is hardly the human way of things. The church often yields quietly, reaching for a sword to defend itself or even to force its own will on reluctant others. It forgets that those outside the faith can be saved only when the church risks itself in faithful weakness. God's people have launched or at least supported wars, perpetuated racism, and propped up numerous unjust political systems. In trying to avoid the counter-cultural tension of its own faith that the scandalous Jesus set in motion, it thereby undercuts its own message and mission. According to Jesus, it is necessary for the church to accept an earthly mission that finds life by giving it away. Believers are caught between truths, finding all by giving all, dying on the way to finally living. Hoping for heaven must never be separated from doing on earth the redeeming will of God.

Jesus found a religious establishment led by people who went through the right religious motions, while they themselves were blind and dead on the inside. Likewise, we find the Christian church too often perishing in the rigidity of some noble liturgy, usually at the hands of leaders who encase in the corridors of a churchly museum some ancient spiritual tradition that once throbbed with life. This is hardly the style of a pilgrim people carrying in their hardened, humbled, and trembling hands the divine seeds of the future! Eternal life, the bloodstream of the church, means being really alive. It is contagious. It constantly finds ways of removing chains, altering circumstances, even opening tombs, always changing the present by the power of God's future.

Jesus said, "Upon this rock I will build my church, and the gates of hell shall not prevail against it" (Matt. 16:18). Most Christians understand this as picturing the church successfully on the defensive, a divine fortress that will never collapse in the face of any assaulting foe. But this is too static and defensive a posture. Christ thought of His disciples as on mission. The believing community is to be on the *offensive*. The gates of hell, not the gates of the church, are being stormed. The good news is that the gates of hell cannot always be impervious to the onslaughts of divine love. No gate need remain shut permanently if the redemptive fellowship of Christ's new people is sufficiently faithful to its marching orders!

A good definition of the Christian church can be constructed from unusual uses of "to be." The church is that body of believers who are dedicated to being an advancing actualization of the *is-ness* of the *shall be*. Believers participate now in that toward which they point. The kingdom of God is *already* and *not yet*. It is that in which we now live and for which we yet wait. It is our hope and our task. It is both an accomplishment and a gift. We work. We wait. We live between the times as we find ourselves caught up in a tension between the age to come and the present evil age.

The reality of the future once penetrated the present. Jeremiah was under palace arrest in Jerusalem while the Babylonian warriors were clamoring outside the walls (Jer. 32:6-15). The city was doomed. The land was already overrun. And what was Jeremiah doing? He was buying a piece of property, as though a real estate transaction was sensible in the midst of his country's total collapse! It was a prophetic action. Jeremiah was able to see the triumph of a distant tomorrow. For him, by faith, tomorrow was already present, at least enough for him to act daringly.

What good did Jesus really do with his loving, integrity, faithfulness, and sacrificial death? Being mocked on a criminal's cross seemed even more useless and tragic than Jeremiah's land purchase. The answer is that there was no *obvious* good. But, in Jesus, tomorrow was already happening. Not obvious to the public eye, God's own future was breaking into human life with an Easter power that eventually will be all in all. The resulting challenge to the church is clear. The church is to buy options on God's future! It must not sit and merely wait. It must not be overwhelmed by the forces of evil and retreat into a protective shell. It must be God's colony in this present world, agents of love, justice, and peace who carry the marks of God's future. The future belongs to God. In the meantime, God's people are blessed to live out of an eternal hope. Now we know in part. We often are *caught between truths*, those of knowing and not knowing, thus living by faith.

Lines written by Adelaide Anne Procter say it well. Someone's fingers wander idly on a piano keyboard. The white and black keys of life jangle together in apparent meaninglessness. But one day God will guide all things and a beautiful chord will sound from a selected group of notes. It will be a "harmonious echo from our discordant life." When Christ returns for his faithful church, he who is the unity of all origins and destinies will speak the words of ultimate and final wisdom. The music of the eternities will sound, linking "all perplexed meanings into one perfect peace."[23]

Look around you. Think of your commitment to God and neighbor, and your membership in God's church. This should be the day *when tomorrow happens*—through you! Here is the precious paradox of Christian mission. The church should be nothing short of that fellowship of *tomorrow's* people who are sharing with Christ the urgent task of rearranging the realities of *today's* world. Then, someday, with time behind us, eternity before us, and the redeemed of all ages around us, there will be heaven, our final and forever home.

Notes

1. Stanley Hauerwas and William H. Willimon, *Resident Aliens: Life in the Christian Colony* (Nashville: Abingdon Press, 1989).

2. Gilbert W. Stafford, *Theology for Disciples* (Anderson, IN: Warner Press, 1996), 307.

3. Seattle Pacific University, Seattle, Washington. This school is associated with the Free Methodist Church.

4. Gilbert W. Stafford, *Theology for Disciples* (Anderson, Ind.: Warner Press, 1996), 3-5.

5. Michael Kinnamon, *Truth and Community* (Grand Rapids: Eerdmans, 1988), 118.

6. Reinhold Niebuhr, *An Interpretation of Christian Ethics* (London: SCM Press, 1948), 151.

7. Robert Webber, *Ancient-Future Faith* (Grand Rapids: Baker Books, 1999).

8. *The Works of the Rev. John Wesley* (London: John Mason, 1856), Vol. XIV, 305.

9. Clouse, Linder, and Pierard, *The Cross & The Flag* (Carol Stream, Illinois: Creation House, 1972), 10.

10. Ronald J. Sider, *The Scandal of the Evangelical Conscience* (Grand Rapids: Baker Books, 2005), 95.

11. As quoted by Mary Bosanquet, *The Life and Death of Dietrich Bonhoeffer* (New York: Harper & Row, 1968), 150.

12. *Newsweek* (May 7, 1973), 12.

13. Benjamin E. Mays, *Born to Rebel* (New York: Charles Scribner's Sons, 1971), 113, 243.

14. Carl F. H. Henry and W. Stanley Mooneyham, editors, *One Race, One Gospel, One Task* (Minneapolis: World Wide Publications, 1967), 16.

15. Stanley Hauerwas and William Willimon, *Resident Aliens* (Nashville: Abingdon Press, 1989), 48.

16. Stanley J. Grenz, *Renewing the Center* (Grand Rapids: Baker Academic, 2000), 299.

17. Barry L. Callen, *Faithful in the Meantime* (Nappanee, IN: Evangel Publishing House, 1997).

18. From the poem "Bar Time" by Billy Collins, in *Sailing Alone Around the Room* (New York: Random House, 2001), 14.

19. John Bright, *A History of Israel* (Philadelphia: The Westminster Press, 1959), 278.

20. Howard A. Snyder, *The Community of the King* (Downers Grove, Ill.: InterVarsity Press, rev. ed. 2004), 59.

21. Brian McClaren, *The Secret Message of Jesus*, (Nashville: W Publishing Group, 2006), 66.

22. McClaren, *The Secret Message of Jesus*, 70.

23. From the poem "A Lost Chord" by Adelaide Anne Procter.

Afterword

Regarding religious truth, it is human to know and not to know for sure. The biblical message is fixed; but how best to explain and apply it is fluid. We are caught between these two truths. The tension need not be disabling, but it is demanding.

The Foreword to this book affirms a particularly strong conviction of D. Elton Trueblood. We Christians need "clear thinking" since the faith we prize "cannot endure by mere organization or by emphasis upon feeling, and little else." We have sought in these chapters to do some clear thinking. We have affirmed the important truth of the *fullness* of the central paradoxes that constitute the Christian faith. Spiritual feelings are fine; however, clear thoughts are better as a solid foundation for faith. Even clear thinking, however, encounters key paradoxes that must be understood and affirmed *in their entirety*. Handling these paradoxes with care is a crucial challenge before the Christian can believe rightly and act wisely.

Numerous influential voices are now being highly critical of any supposed universals in religion. They oppose any norms, values, or standards claimed to be absolutely true for all people, times, and places. Religious fundamentalisms are particular targets of the criticism, and understandably so given the violence around the world practiced by people in the name of their beliefs. The current call is to reject the control of all religious traditions on the wider public.

This caution against religious absolutes is appropriate to a point. Believers can get very detailed in their doctrinal claims and insist rather arrogantly that all of what they believe is absolutely true, for them and everyone else who is not deluded by unbelief. Despite the tendency to arrogance, the question remains. Is anything really true, absolutely true, true for everyone regardless of time or place? With all appropriate cautions recognized, I still risk an affirmative answer, if by "absolute" is meant that there are truths which are unsurpassably true.

The word absolute is a creation of modern philosophy and means quite literally that something is unique because it is "unrelated" and stands by itself all alone in isolation from everything else. It was a term primarily used in modern thought by deists and pantheists in speaking of God. This is why I think we should use considerable caution in using this term. Nonetheless, there are unsurpassable truths—although they are relatively few in number.

I have affirmed in these pages that God exists, is truly sovereign over all, is unchanging in nature, and is understood best in Jesus. I wish to conclude this book by identifying and exploring briefly two sets of observations on biblical teaching that I believe provide divinely revealed and thus dependable guidelines for Christian faith. These guidelines assist our understanding of God's historic revelation and our applying of it to ever-changing circumstances. They are not laid on the Bible, but emerge out of the Bible itself. Not surprisingly, they are not without their own paradoxical dimensions, nor are they the kinds of church doctrine and systematic theology that many Christians often insist upon. Nevertheless, they are definite enough to be helpful as Christians pursue the fullness of biblical truth without overstating their truth claims.

Guidelines: Set One

Biblical writers appear to have employed several theological guidelines as they themselves had to relate the biblical tradition they already knew to new and often perplexing circumstances.[1] To be the believer God intends, these guidelines are to be understood and lived out *together*—to break their paradoxical interconnectivity is to lose vital focus. Specifically:

1. Biblical writers "monotheized" the ideas they encountered ansometimes borrowed from the cultures around them. There is only one God. Idolatry in all of its subtle forms is intolerable. This includes the tendency of people of faith to focus too much on their own thinking, traditions, and perceived needs. All is to be believed and done for the glory of the one God. This God is understood best in Jesus Christ, with the goal of the life of faith being to grow up into the image of Christ. *God is one and is known best in Jesus.*

2. Biblical writers recognized with gratitude that God functions as loving grace, with such graciousness bringing into being a special

faith community, Israel and then the church. The purpose of God's people is the divine mission in this world. The one God has called together one people to be a special treasure and an instrument of the divine mission. To be "saved" is to be a transformed and empowered part of the divine people on mission. Christian faith is less about "me" and more about "us" as we are changed and sent by God into the world. *God has a special people among whom humans are privileged to find their fullest identity and purpose in life.*

3. Biblical writers cautioned against an inordinate, prideful focus on even the special people of God. When arrogance replaces gratitude, God's people are distracted from the larger truth, which is that God loves all people in all dimensions of their lives. God's love "requires that we pay attention to issues of social, structural sin, and questions of justice. Our faith must be both demystified and deprivatized; salvation is deeply personal, but never merely private."[2] *God loves and offers redemption for all people in all of their lives.*

4. Biblical writers went beyond realizing that the divine love is lavished on a blessed people. It is supposed to be shared by that people with all of the world. They realized that God's love often focuses on the great needs of the poor, weak, and dispossessed. Said Jesus, reflecting an emphasis in his own Jewish tradition: "And the king will answer them, 'Truly I tell you, just as you did it to one of the least of these who are members of my family, you did it to me'" (Matt. 25:40). *God has a caring eye especially focused on the poor—and so should his church.*

5. Biblical writers were amazed that God works in and even throughhuman sin and error to accomplish divine purposes. God is at work even in *you* and *me*, common sinners being saved by grace. Therefore, we should be patient with the failings of others and the embarrassments sometimes seen in church life, both now and in the past. We know that "all things work together for good for those who love God, who are called according to his purpose" (Rom. 8:28). *God is now at work wonderfully in the midst of this corrupt world, and even in our less-than-ideal congregations of Christians.*

Guidelines: Set Two

The following guidelines go beyond the basic biblical teachings listed in Set One. They assist believers in adapting the expressions and implications of these beliefs to new times and places, without violating their enduring integrity. If (1) there is only one God, (2) God is known most fully in Jesus Christ, and (3) God is reaching out to all people in love, then interpreting Jesus to new generations of people in changing cultures is a major challenge of utmost importance.

New Testament writers were already about this ongoing mission process. For instance, there are four Gospels in the New Testament, not just one. There is "an inherent pluralism in the phenomenon of four gospels which allows them to function in an inspirational and fertile way for different kinds of people and in different kinds of circumstances."[3] They each sought to explain the person of Jesus Christ in settings sharply different from that of the biblical tradition. John Howard Yoder surveyed five of these explanations of Jesus as they are found in Colossians 1, Philippians 2, John 1, Hebrews, and Revelation 5.[4] He found that inside the New Testament there are differing (not *conflicting*) ways to conceive and explain the person and work of Jesus.

Each of these New Testament explanations brings the story of Jesus to a prevailing belief system of the world and seeks to demonstrate in that system's environment who Jesus really is for them. The New Testament explanations resonate with the theological foundations of Set One above and share a common "deep structure" as they face a given challenge in its distinctive way. This deep structure recognizes both the inevitable variety of thinking within the Christian community and the belief elements that are *always necessary* if that community is to be its distinctive self.

The deep structure that is common to all biblical explanations of Jesus, and thus is larger than any one of them, consists of six elements. Christian believers must be able and willing to...

1. Become at home in new linguistic worlds and be willing to use their languages and face their questions. Christians must be *in the world* in order to address it meaningfully.

2. Place Jesus above and in charge of the cosmos rather than fit the message about him into the lesser slot that the new thought worlds are prepared to create for it. Christians must be willing to confront the world with the *absolute claim* of Jesus.

3. Identify the lordship of Jesus Christ by putting focus on the rejection and suffering experienced by Jesus in human form. Christians must accept the *sharp contrast* of their Jesus message with usual human expectations of the divine.

4. Recognize that "salvation" is not yielding to some pre-set ritual or thought system designed by any human culture. Christians must affirm, in the manner of Jesus, that salvation is entering into a *self-emptying and death*. By God's grace alone, people share in the glorious resurrection of the Son.

5. Affirm that, behind the cosmic victory of Jesus, lies belief in the pre-existence of Christ (he was before creation was), meaning that Jesus Christ is nothing less than *co-essential with the Father* and a prime participant in creation and providence.

6. Teach that all readers of these several New Testament explanations of Jesus can now *share by faith* in the wonderful implications of the victory of Jesus over all sin and evil.

No one of the ways of explaining the person and work of Jesus is the exclusive one in itself. The New Testament presents several and allows them to stand beside each other. Isolated from the others, any one suffers a significant inadequacy. Each shares a common historical base, set of themes and discipleship implications, and assumes the elements of the biblical "deep structure." The language and images may shift with changing settings, but all explanations should remain anchored to "the astounding claim of the Christian story," namely that "through this man, Jesus of Nazareth, God has definitively manifested himself. In Jesus Christ, the God of the universe is uniquely present and working in history among us, as validated by the resurrection from the dead."[5]

While the biblical anchor must hold in the midst of cross-cultural evangelism (Set One), the conflicting mind-sets of the world's cultures are to be addressed in ways understandable to them—but without sacrificing the priority of the Jewish tradition and the Jesus reality (Set Two). Instead of "requesting free speech and room for one more stand in the Athenian marketplace of ideas, the biblical writer's claim was that now the Hebrew story had widened out to include everyone."[6] The story remains true, even while its thought structures and language shift to keep clear communication alive.

Here is a key paradox not to be violated. The church is not called to accept and fit its Jesus message into the limits of the world's thought, although addressing such thought meaningfully is always necessary. Doctrine is important in the life of Christian faith. However, theological language is always inadequate. What, then, can serious Christian believers count on without question? We have sought to identify in these pages a range of core truths, often balanced elements of central paradoxes that are basic to Christian faith in all places and times. This Afterword has added two sets of biblical guidelines that are dependable guides to believing and evangelizing.

We Christians may be caught *between truths*, but *truths there are*! The call is to be *whole* in our thinking. We are to listen as well as speak, thinking and living humbly and courageously. We are to rejoice in the goodness of the gracious God who is both biblically revealed and yet beyond our full knowing. To be caught in this *knowing-unknowing* is to be human; to grasp it by faith and live it to the full is to be blessed forever!

Notes

1. James A Sanders, *Canon and Community* (Philadelphia: Fortress Press, 1984), 51.

2. Clark M. Williamson, *Way of Blessing, Way of Life* (St. Louis: Chalice Press, 1999), 31.

3. Stephen C. Barton, *The Spirituality of the Gospels* (Peabody, Mass.: Hendrickson Publishers, 1992), 147.

4. John Howard Yoder, *The Priestly Kingdom* (Notre Dame, Ind.: University of Notre Dame Press, 1984), 50ff.

5. Clark H. Pinnock, *Tracking the Maze* (N.Y.: Harper & Row, 1990), 197-198.

6. Yoder, *op. cit.*, 54.

Index of Subjects and Persons

A
absolutes 131
affirmation 65, 96–97
Allen, C. Leonard 14, 83
Allison, Joseph (backcover)
ambiguity 80
Anselm, 49
apostolic 109
artist 96
atonement 76
authority 66

B
Baillie, D. M. 68, 83
baptism of the Spirit 81
Barclay, William 39–40, 105
Barton, Stephen C. 136
belief 9–11, 63, 70–71, 80, 116, 134–135
Berle, Milton 86, 105
Bible 10–12, 68, 74, 80, 89–91, 109, 118, 122, 124, 132
block logic 11
Bloesch, Donald 83
body 86, 88–89, 107–108, 110, 111–112, 114, 122, 125, 127
body-souls 89
Bonhoeffer, Dietrich 86, 95, 105–106, 121, 128
Book of Revelation 105, 117
Bright, John 100, 129
Byron, Lord 86

C
Caesar 114, 117, 123
Caesarea Philippi 65, 113
Callen, Barry L. 7, 8, 83, 106, 128
Carver, Frank 106
catholic 109, 111–12

charismatic 113
Chesterton, G. K. 10, 14
Christendom 122
Christian perfection 116
Christ-likeness 109
church 9–13, 64–65, 67, 70, 72, 76, 80–81, 83, 96–97, 105, 107–28, 132–33, 136
churches 10, 110
civil disobedience 118
Collins, Billy 105, 115, 129
colony of heaven 109
complexity of truth 8
conflict 90, 113
conversion 100–101, 116, 121
creeds 12, 67
criticism 72, 131
Crosby, Fanny J. 74, 83
cross 67, 71, 76–78, 83, 87, 97, 127–28, 135
crucifixion of Jesus 67, 87
cruciform church 76, 83

D
Daniel 118
deists 132
denominations 110
devil 77
Dialogues of Plato 25
diffusion, philosophy of 114
diversity 12–13, 125
doctrine 63, 65, 78, 80–81, 99, 118, 123, 132, 136
Dostoevsky, Fedor 86
double-talk 80
doubt 86
dualism 87
Durocher, Leo 91

E
Easter 71, 100, 109, 127
ecology 110
ecumenical movement 13
ecumenism 13
election 11, 95
Elijah-Elisha paradox 119–120
Erasmus 104, 106

eschatology 104, 106, 124
evangelical 12–14, 111, 118, 120, 128
evangelism 117, 122, 135
evil 75, 77, 86–92, 112, 117–19, 122, 125, 127, 135
exile 71, 122
exodus from Egypt 71, 115

F
faith 7, 10, 13–14, 63–64, 67–70, 72, 74, 77, 79, 80–81, 83, 85–86, 90, 94, 96, 99, 100, 102–103, 106–109, 111–116, 118–24, 126–28, 131–133, 135–36
fall of humankind 100
fanaticism 10
flesh 67, 69, 74, 81, 88–90, 105

G
Golgotha 76
gospel 10, 70, 72, 99, 102, 107, 114–17, 121, 123, 128
government 111, 117–18, 125
grace 65, 68, 73, 76, 78, 82–83, 90, 92–104, 108, 112, 115, 118, 122, 132–133, 135
grass-god beings 87
Greek philosophic concepts 89
Grenz, Stanley J., 60, 128

H
Hatfield, Mark 118
Hauerwas, Stanley 128
heaven 67, 70, 73, 92, 107– 112, 114, 122, 124–26, 128
Hebrews 11, 63, 116, 134
Henry, Carl F. H. 122, 128
Herodians 125
high and nigh 71, 75
holiness 73, 82, 88, 92, 116
holy 65, 73–74, 78–79, 81–83, 85, 99, 100, 114, 116, 119, 122, 125
hope 88, 93, 95, 102, 104–105, 114, 116, 123, 125, 127
human history 66, 115–17, 124
humility 7, 11, 82

I
idolatry 71, 73, 117, 120, 132
image of God 90–91, 93
immanence 81
impossible possibility 99, 100

incarnation 69, 70, 78
inspiration 109
intellectual integrity 7
intellectual rigor 7
intercessory prayer 75
interlocking necessities 109
Isaiah 82, 87, 124

J
Jerusalem 66, 114, 119, 127
Jochebed 118
justice 76, 87, 116–17, 122, 127, 133

K
Kennedy, John F. 80
King, Martin Luther, Jr. 121
kingdom of God 64, 123–27
Kinnamon, Michael 14, 128
knowing-unknowing 82, 136
knowledge 70, 73, 82, 92, 105, 112

L
Lambeth Conference 99
language 78, 92, 135–36
law 77, 92–94, 98
license 94, 98
Lincoln, Abraham 8
logic 11, 68, 78
love 13, 63–64, 67–69, 71, 73–74, 76, 78, 80–83, 87–88, 91–93, 95, 97–101, 114–16, 122, 125, 126–127, 133, 134
Luther, Martin 64, 69, 82, 94, 118

M
Macquarrie, John 49, 60
magician 96
McLaren, Brian 106
Mays, Benjamin 121, 128
membership, church 10, 107, 111–12, 128
metaphors 77
Micah 124
miracles of Jesus 66
mission 10, 68, 82, 102, 105–106, 109, 112–17, 120–24, 126, 128, 133–34
monastic 96
Moses 118

musical score 69
mystery 63–64, 67, 77, 94, 110, 125
mystical 96

N
negation 96
Niebuhr, Reinhold 87, 105, 113, 118, 128

O
Old Testament 11, 73
Olson, Roger 14
original sin 93
orthodoxy, critical and generous 12–14, 29, 37, 106
orthodoxy, romance of 10, 14
orthopraxy 29

P
parables 26, 28
paradox 7–11, 13, 15, 18, 21, 27, 30–32, 42–43, 45, 50–51, 55, 57, 59, 63–64, 69–70, 72, 74–76, 78–79, 82, 85, 87–88, 93, 95, 97, 98–99, 105, 112–13, 115–16, 119–20, 123–126, 128, 136
Pascal, Blaise 20, 34, 38, 85
patience 11–13, 21, 33, 36, 49, 64
Paul 32, 41, 45, 48, 58, 65, 68, 77, 79, 82, 86, 89–90, 94–95, 98–99, 102, 110, 114, 120, 125
pentecostalism 10
perfect love 92
Peter 48, 67, 87, 98, 100, 110, 113, 118
Pharisees 125
piecemealism 23
pietism 10
Pinnock, Clark H. 14, 61, 82–83, 136
pluralism 20, 134
pneuma 89
poetry 28–29, 56, 95
polarities of Christian experience 23
politics 10, 80, 89, 118, 121
postmodernism 19, 37, 60
Powell, Samuel M. 105
power 23, 43–44, 51, 56, 58, 69, 73–74, 76–78, 81, 92, 99, 104, 109, 112, 114, 117, 119–20, 124–27
predestination 11, 95
Procter, Adelaide Anne 127, 129
proofs 19

protestant 23, 109, 118
Protestant Reformation 118
purity of heart 94

Q
quadrilateral 45–46, 60

R
Rahab 118
rationalism 12, 44, 47, 49
reason 12, 15, 19–20, 27, 42–49, 53, 63, 67, 87–88, 90
reductionist tactics 36
religion 7–8, 26, 30, 37, 41, 47, 51, 60, 72, 99, 113, 116, 120–21, 131
resident aliens 60, 107, 122–23, 128
resurrection 22, 65, 70, 74, 76, 78–79, 125, 135
reverence 7, 29, 71, 73
riddle 64, 80
righteousness 90, 92, 121
risk 18, 52–53, 63, 74, 131
ritual 135
Roman Empire 98, 120, 125
Rossetti, Christina 75

S
Saducees 125
Saint Francis of Assisi 23
saints 41, 65, 73, 107
salvation 21, 42, 57, 59, 71–72, 74, 76–77, 87, 93, 95, 97–99, 102–103, 111, 116–117, 121, 123, 133, 135
sanctification 92
Sanders, James A. 136
sarx 89–90
scholars 17, 58
Schweitzer, Albert 67, 83
science 18, 30, 37, 44, 47
scientific method 44
segregation 121
sentimentalizing 72, 73
separation of church and state 118
Sermon on the Mount 99, 121
sexuality 89–90
Shaw, Bernard 92
Sider, Ronald J. 60, 128
sin 18, 20, 44, 70, 72, 77, 79, 82, 88–93, 97–98, 102, 133, 135

slavery 89, 94, 97–98, 121
Snyder, Howard A. 129
social holiness 116
sociology 112
Socrates 8, 25–26
soma 89
soul 18, 27, 35, 44–45, 50, 66, 89
sovereignty, divine 22, 73, 75–76, 81
Spirit 15, 21, 24, 29, 46–47, 50–51, 56, 58–60, 65, 78–79, 81–82, 85, 88,
    89–90, 100–101, 105, 109, 112–113, 119, 124–25
Spirit of Christ 59, 79, 90, 101
Spirit of God 21, 58–59, 60, 113
spiritual 10, 18–19, 26, 37, 42, 44, 46, 50, 54–55, 60, 65, 68, 73–74, 87, 89,
    96, 102, 104, 107, 113, 117, 119, 121–22, 126, 131
Spivak, Lawrence 80
St. Augustine 94–95, 106
Stagg, Frank 83
Stafford, Gilbert W. 128
Staples, Rob 106
suffering 40, 69, 76, 135
superstitions 44
Sweet, Leonard 19, 37
symbol 63, 113

T
Tale of Two Cities 33
technology 20
Temple, William 24, 49, 60
tenses of salvation 102
the world 114
theological equilibrium 12, 24, 25
theologies, unbalanced 12, 16, 43, 55, 111
theology 10–14, 16, 19, 24–26, 28, 35, 40–41, 53–55, 60–61, 64, 65, 74, 80,
    83, 89, 92, 105, 128, 132
Thielicke, Helmut 53
Thorsen, Don 60
Thurman, Howard 50, 61
Tillich, Paul 106
tradition, tradition 12, 46, 80
transcendence 28, 81
Trinity 44, 63, 65, 78, 80–81
tri-theism 80
Trueblood, David Elton 7–8, 24, 37, 48, 60, 102, 105–106, 131
truth 8, 10–37, 42–56, 59–60, 63–70, 72–73, 77–78, 80–81, 87, 90, 94,
    109, 111–13, 115, 120, 123, 128, 131–33

tuning fork, principle of 31

U
unity 13, 35, 36, 57, 80, 111, 128
universal 49, 65, 79, 113

V
Van Zanten, John 33
virgin birth 41
vocational 96

W
Ware, Bishop Kallistos 29, 37
Webber, Robert E. 106, 116, 128
Wesley, Charles 60–61
Wesley, John 40, 92, 116, 121, 128
Westminster Shorter Catechism 92
Whitehead, Alfred North 31, 37
Williamson, Clark M. 136
Wilson, Marvin 14, 37
wisdom 9, 11–13, 25–27, 33, 35–36, 42, 44–45, 47, 49, 56, 58–59, 63, 67, 80, 92, 95, 112, 127
With Head and Heart 50, 61
Wood, Laurence W. (backcover)
Word-Spirit combination 60
works 59, 97–98, 99, 133
worship 66, 68, 73, 78, 81, 111, 114, 119

Y
yes-and-no beings 90
yesterday-today-tomorrow 116
Yoder, John Howard 134, 136

Z
Zealots 125

About the Author

Barry L. Callen holds earned doctoral degrees from Chicago Theological Seminary and Indiana University, with masters degrees from Anderson University School of Theology and Asbury Theological Seminary. Currently, he is University Professor of Christian Studies Emeritus at Anderson University and editor of both Anderson University Press (since 2000) and the *Wesleyan Theological Journal* (since 1992). He has authored more than thirty books, including: *Radical Christianity* (1999); *Journey Toward Renewal: An Intellectual Biography of Clark H. Pinnock* (2000); *Authentic Spirituality* (2001, 2006); *Discerning the Divine* (2004); and *The Scripture Principle*, with Clark Pinnock (2006). An ordained minister of the Church of God (Anderson), Dr. Callen has served as dean of both the undergraduate college and graduate seminary of Anderson University. Having taught Christian theology for many years, he now serves as Special Assistant to the General Director of Church of God Ministries and is editor of his church's *Ministerial Credentials Manual*.

Because this writer is a mature scholar with deep roots in the ongoing life of the church, *Caught Between Truths* is both well informed theologically and dedicated to the pressing needs of thoughtful Christians seeking perspective and balance in their believing.

www.ingramcontent.com/pod-product-compliance
Lightning Source LLC
Chambersburg PA
CBHW021145230426
43667CB00005B/258